NEWBEE

Lessons Learned while Cross-Pollinating my Life,
Discovering my Passions, and Creating my Honey

ERNESTO MANDOWSKY

For ordering details on mass quantities,
contact hello@crosspollinationdesign.com

First Edition.

Print ISBN: 978-1-73549-600-9
eBook ISBN: 978-1-73549-601-6

www.ernestomandowsky.com
www.thenewbeebook.com

Dedicated to the Weak who help us find Strength

"Why would the desert reveal such things to a stranger, when it knows that we have been here for generations?" said another of the chieftains.

"Because my eyes are not yet accustomed to the desert," the boy said. "I can see things that eyes habituated to the desert might not see."

—Excerpt from Paulo Coelho's *The Alchemist*

CONTENTS

HOW I GOT HERE

Three years ago, I started writing this book. Or maybe it was over a decade ago, when I thought I knew what I wanted to do with my life. Coaching basketball, opening restaurants, creating technology, the list goes on and on.

Through trial and error, I tried to make sense of the various interests that pulled me in all sorts of directions. As I moved through my journey, I discovered new paths that continued to change my trajectory. Or so I thought.

Originally, I set out to write a book about how the restaurant world needed outsiders to bring their unique experiences into the industry. As I continued to draft the pages, I realized that the story was much larger than just the food world.

Wines and spirits acquire their complex flavors through an intricate aging process, which starts with a number of steps to begin fermentation. Once settled in carefully designed barrels, the passage of time is what enables these products to develop their intricate flavor profiles. *NewBee* is the evolution of my originally intended work, aged by personal reflection on my journey to date.

This book is about exploring our environments, discovering what feeds our curiosity, and cross-pollinating our future.

Thank you for supporting my project,

Ernesto Mandowsky

AN INTRODUCTION TO CROSS-POLLINATION

Like many of my millennial amigos, I had no idea what I was going to do growing up. Instead of picking a singular path, I was more curious to find a way to do it all. I've always had a number of interests and passions. *How can I combine all of my interests and passions into a rewarding career experience?* I have had this question on my mind for as long as I can remember. I relied on an unapologetic approach in searching for answers—asking the universe.

When I was headed to college, family members started asking me about my future. *Are you going to pursue finance, law, or medicine?* Having had a few encounters with hospitality in my teen years, I became interested in the restaurant world. *What kind of shmuck are you? Don't you know that 90 percent of restaurants fail?* What a supportive group of loved ones I had.

I'm an engineer. I know the statistics. I loved what restaurants represented, and I've also always been a bit of a contrarian—have you seen my glasses? They are bright orange—not the typical choice of color to complement your face.

I never followed paths that were already laid out—my academic interests were not in finance, medicine, or law, which were what my family and communities subtly tried to encourage me to pursue. Even when it came to entering the hospitality world, I couldn't choose the road less traveled, because there wasn't any road to begin with. I wanted to apply systems engineering theory to the world of food and beverages, a nonexistent path (as far as I knew).

At school, there was no major called restaurant analytics, no student organizations tailored to hospitality technology, no conferences where professionals would network and share the latest kitchen innovations for restaurants. While working in a restaurant as a busboy, I often asked about how technology could be used to streamline the chaotic environment. When I brought up my ideas with my managers, I was shut down and told to get back to work. I hoped that I would have better luck with these conversations after moving to New York, one of the hospitality capitals of the world, and asking hospitality professionals how to pursue my interests. They'd never heard of someone who wanted to apply systems engineering to the restaurant world. Their recommendation was to start at the bottom and learn the business by washing dishes or busing tables. Starting from the bottom is usually how it goes. However, I'd tried that. My bottom was different from theirs. Actually, everyone's bottom is.

Maybe I wasn't clear, or maybe my audience didn't understand how to guide me toward my goal, which I guess seemed *out there*. With an ego that was constantly attempting to destroy my self-esteem by reminding me that I had no idea what I was doing, I had to persist and remain focused on answering my life's question of combining my interests and curiosities into a rewarding career experience.

I didn't realize it at the time, but I was trying to *cross-pollinate*. I was trying to combine two interests in a way that was not easily understood by an audience trapped in their own worldview, shaped by their narrow set of experiences. Since the first steps of my journey were not clearly obvious, I needed to create them.

My hospitality journey began with an obsession, literally. After overcoming a medically diagnosed eating disorder, I reoriented my relationship with food, recognizing its ability to bring people together. Meeting a restaurateur led me to discover a potential career path where I could use the power of food and hospitality to do that. But how would I reconcile that with my choice of studying systems engineering in college? My major didn't offer as clear a path to restaurant ownership as it did to other engineering-focused vocations. While I spent five years taking classes in computer programming, lean manufacturing production systems, and analytical methods to improve engineering systems, I was really learning how to answer my question on how to create a career experience made up of my various interests.

Outside of class, I met tons of like-minded individuals who would teach me how to lead student organizations, bake bread, start food companies, and develop relationships. By weaving all of these experiences together, I slowly began creating my own nontraditional path. With small victories, I started to convince myself that it was possible to combine multiple interests to create a rewarding, *cross-pollinated* career experience.

While celebrating my quarter-life crisis, I read an article about bees and honey. I realized the similarity with what I had been doing throughout all these years. Bees explore their environments, searching for flowers to extract nectar, and then carry it back to the hive for the housekeeping bees to make honey. As the bees go from flower to flower, they are also transferring pollen, which enables the flowers to reproduce through their natural cycles. For years, I had been extracting lessons and insights by volunteering in organizations, attending conferences, reading books, working in jobs, interacting with mentors, and taking courses. By combining all of these takeaways from the different flowers along my journey, I've created my own honey—a unique combination of insights and skills that I can offer to the world, the restaurant world, in my case.

NewBee is my story, meant to show others how they can cross-pollinate their lives. It is the stories of the flowers from my fields that resulted in the combs that make up my honey. While the book contains my specific episodes with restaurants, technology, and education, my intention is that you look past the specifics and understand the lessons that can be applied across industries and areas of focus. While some people do have more of a traditional path laid out for them, exploring alternative worlds may enable them to discover innovative ways to create a career experience that is unique to them, standing out from the crowd. This book is aimed at people with a diverse array of eclectic interests— writing, video production, computers, sales, media, education, activism, crafts—who are facing external or internal pressure to follow a well-marked path. It is meant to show them that it is possible incorporate all these eclectic interests into their own unique career path.

While millennials are criticized for their fleeting loyalty as they jump from job to job, *NewBee* celebrates the limitless possibilities that society has created for us to manifest our deepest desires, intertwining them into our personal and professional lives.

I hope my story inspires you to identify the flowers around you, to cross-pollinate your life, and to create your unique, one-of-a-kind honey.

CHAPTER ONE
It Starts with Attraction

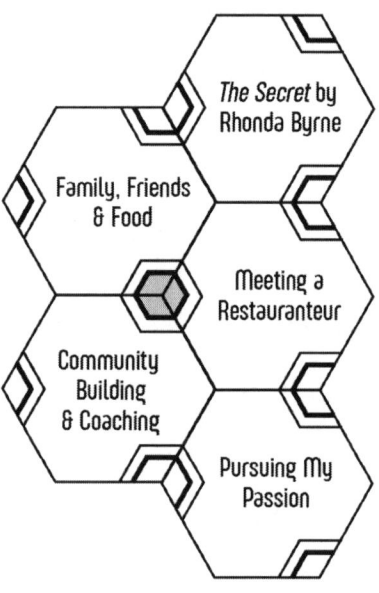

The Secret by Rhonda Byrne

Family, Friends & Food

Meeting a Restauranteur

Community Building & Coaching

Pursuing My Passion

When I was a child, I viewed my parents as my heroes and teachers—the be-all and end-all when it came to anything about how life worked. Their lessons were absolute truths. However, as I got older, my perspective started to change. I guess that's part of the whole adolescent rebellious phase. I relied on their teachings less and less, feeling overly confident about life. It was around this time that my grandma would start calling me "Mr. I Know."

During junior year, my friends started talking about their futures. They discussed the colleges they planned to visit, the majors they were interested in, and what their postgraduation plans were. These conversations got me thinking: Where was I going to go to school? What was I going to do with my life? They seemed to have had it all figured out, and I didn't even know where to begin. I was lost.

Realizing I was more "Mr. Know Nothing," than "Mr. I Know," I had to turn to the only people who might be able to help me think about my future: my parents. This was going to be tough. Not only did we never speak about this topic, but I knew that they had had a completely different vantage point when they were in my shoes. They didn't have a choice where they wanted to study. They went to the universities near their families in South America, which had a completely different school system than the United States. How was I supposed to take their advice when they didn't have the slightest clue on navigating the American university system? How were we supposed to even start talking about my future, when my view was completely different from theirs?

Attraction

My parents taught me key lessons that would be far superior to the advice I thought I needed about college. They taught me the principles that would become my guiding tools to figure out all my life's questions.

My mother taught me the importance of working incredibly hard to develop and maintain connections with friends, colleagues, and clients. As a travel agent, she helped people get from A to B, serving executives of global companies who traveled across three continents. Her clients loved her not only for her guidance on how to travel efficiently but for her ability to suggest restaurants, hotels, and must-see attractions that would greatly enrich their trips. Her constant focus on public relations is what enabled her to bring our family around the world. I attributed our ability to travel to the connections she created with her clients. *Take care of your network* was a value taught to me early on.

My father taught me a very different set of skills. He taught me about personal transformation through dreaming and visualization. As an architect, my dad conceives ideas, drafts floorplans and sketches, and then actually builds them. Although not interested in architecture, I was fascinated to learn how to imagine and manifest my own wishes. These lessons began on a rainy Sunday afternoon when I was sixteen years old.

"Hey, do you want to watch this movie?" my father asked me.

"Sure, what is it about?"

The movie was titled *The Secret* and was based on the best-selling book by Rhonda Byrne. It was about creating a dream life using a secret power.

For the next hour and a half, we listened to a diverse group of entrepreneurs, doctors, spiritual leaders, quantum physicists, and philosophers describe their interpretation of the secret to creating abundant health, wealth, and success within our lives.

What they were describing is known as the *Law of Attraction* and can be summarized as "thoughts become things." The idea is that the images and pictures that enter the mind eventually become reality. For me, the movie was an introduction to the importance of how maintaining a positive mindset and a focus on your desires can contribute to creating a life of your choosing. I remember thinking: *maybe this will help me figure out what the hell I am going to do with my life.*

As a teenager, I hadn't lived through the circumstances discussed in the movie. I had no idea what balancing the responsibilities of careers, relationships, family, personal health, finances, etc., was like. What I did take away was that you have the power to create a life filled with your hopes and dreams, no matter how intricate they are. That really excited me.

While the whole concept of the Law of Attraction was a bit over my head at the time, one tool I felt that I could immediately start using was a vision board. Creating a vision board, as the movie explains, is the process of curating a set of images, photographs, and phrases describing or illustrating your desires and placing them onto a board. By routinely looking at the board, you generate images of these desires in your mind. The things on your mind become the things in your life. *Thoughts become things.*

So, I began cutting pictures out from magazines to complete my art project. When I finished, I hung the masterpiece above the desk in my room. Every night after finishing my homework, I would stare at the pictures, feeling as if those images had become a part of my reality. This "lite" version had the following: a logo of the University of Florida, one of the schools I wanted to go to; a photo of my family, representing my desire to always be surrounded by loved ones; a check made out for $25,000, the sum of money required to pay for my university studies; and lastly, a picture of me at the Jewish Community Center (or JCC), representing my desire to one day have the same sense of community that I had been blessed with while growing up.

Despite my newly formed ideas about the universe providing whatever ideas I put in my mind, I knew that things weren't just going to appear. If I wanted something, I had to go out and get it myself. The universe would meet me somewhere in the middle—or maybe, like 70 percent of the way there.

How did I come to pick these specific things for my vision board? I could have cut out pictures of "fancy toys" like a sports car, a million-dollar check, or even a yacht. But there would not have been any substance behind these wishes. Rather, I chose representations of the feelings from my favorite memories of my youth that I desired for my future. I wanted to become independent and contribute to my community.

Educating the Community

The JCC was central to my childhood. It was the gathering place for most of the people I knew while growing up. There, I built a tight-knit group of friends playing on various sports teams and volunteering within the youth leadership program. To paint a better picture of what a JCC is, think of a YMCA, a local church, a summer camp, a theater, or your local gym. The JCC was kind of a combination of all of these. After years as a participant in various programs, I shifted to becoming a creator of the community experience at "the J."

Having attended an elementary and middle school next door to the J, it was easy for me to get involved. When I went to high school, I was miles away from the center and had to find transportation to get there every day for basketball practice. Since both my parents worked, and I didn't have friends heading in that direction after school, I would bike five miles every day to get there. My desire to become independent from others to get around town extended to my wish to buy a car one day. Since my parents told me that I would have to pay for it, I needed to find a job and make money. Although the universe didn't give me a winning lottery ticket, it did show me an opportunity to make money once I had placed that intention in my mind.

One day, I was at the J a few hours before my team's basketball practice. When I bumped into the head coach of the children's basketball program, who was also my new coach, he asked me, "Hey, can you help me teach one of the youth classes today?" I thought about it for a moment. Sure, why not? Entering the gym and looking onto the court, I saw the little monsters—I mean children—running all over the place, screaming at the top of their lungs. *Oh Lord,* I thought. Taking a deep breath, I grabbed the extra whistle he had and stepped onto the court. Fede offered me a job to come back and help him out. I guess he believed in me. Early proof of this mysterious secret—for me, at least.

And with that began my four-year stint as an after-school basketball coach. Managing groups of fifty-plus children was no easy feat. At first, it felt incredibly difficult since they had so much energy and could barely pay attention. I also had no idea what I was doing. Class after class, I asked Federico how I could do a better job. He gave me two key pieces of advice. 1) Focus on keeping a positive attitude despite the kids' hyperactivity, and 2) use that same high energy and mirror their behavior during instruction. I implemented his tips and eventually figured out how to instruct them on the fundamentals of the game.

Over the years, I started teaching older children, shifting from individual skills like dribbling and shooting to team-based concepts like passing and moving without the ball. While the biweekly paycheck financially rewarded my efforts, I gained tremendous fulfillment from educating others on concepts that would contribute to their success. Realizing how rewarding this was, I sought out other ways where I could make an impact. Fortunately, the JCC had another opportunity for me.

On the weekends, I volunteered with a youth leadership initiative similar to the Boy and Girl Scouts of America. We used sports and team-building games to teach important cultural lessons to children and teens. Since I was already working with younger kids during the week through basketball, I requested to work with the older groups, the "know-it-all" teenagers. I thought working with hyperactive children was tough. Teenagers came with a whole new set of challenges.

Cell phones and pheromones were two of the most distracting forces ruling these teenagers' lives. I had no idea what I was getting myself into with this new age demographic. Initially struggling to gain their attention and respect, I turned to the program leaders for advice. What they told me was not so different from what Federico had told me a few years prior. I had to keep a positive attitude, not get discouraged, and mirror their behavior. I noticed that their behaviors were heavily influenced by their desire to be active and to mingle with one another; they wanted to flirt.

We created activities that enabled the group to interact through social and athletic games like capture the flag with water balloons, messy Twister with chocolate syrup, hide-and-seek at night, and other games that made it easy for the girls and the guys to socialize. Our tactics were questionable, but I can assure you that everything was kosher. Eventually, my co-counselors and I built a good rapport with the group, many of whom I am still close friends with years later.

The work and volunteer experiences at the JCC taught me how I could use coaching and mentorship as a means to nurture relationships within my community. At home, I became aware of one of the most powerful tools that we used to connect with family and our closest friends.

Family, Friends, and Food

I was born into a family of nomads. My grandparents fled to South America from Europe during World War II, arriving in Peru and Brazil, where my mother and father would eventually be born. My parents would ultimately meet in Miami, get married, and have my brother and me. Throughout my childhood, relatives who lived in other parts of the world would visit, bringing their local cultures with them. With guests from Colombia, France, Switzerland, Venezuela, Argentina, and Brazil, our home became quite the melting pot.

Although we lived so far apart, my aunts and uncles prioritized maintaining a strong bond. We united once or twice a year in Miami, the crossroad between Europe and South America. When they came to visit, we spent our time going to the beach or eating together. (Really, what else can a group of twenty-plus people do easily?) Since restaurants don't typically accommodate groups our size without advanced planning and/or ridiculous reconfigurations of entire sections, we had to flex our creative muscles in the food department. We opted to prepare a majority of our meals at home.

Prior to our meals, we would spend hours buying groceries, cutting up and preparing the food, playing board games or sports outside, and bonding. After eating, we would occasionally break out into dancing samba and singing disco songs from the '70s and '80s right in the living room. Celebratory food experiences were at the core of our family bonding.

Throughout the fifty weeks of the year not spent with our relatives, my parents continued to emphasize the importance of eating together and sharing our culture with close friends. Every night of the week, we dined together as a family, no matter how late Mami and Papi arrived home from work. On Fridays, we practiced the Jewish custom of Shabbat, which featured an elaborately home-cooked meal. Every week, my parents and their friends rotated houses, which offered different environments for the kids to play. Over the years of attending these dinners, I developed very close relationships with them through playing video games, running around the backyard, and gossiping about our lives as we ate.

Years ago, I heard a quote from one of the founders of a global high-end Japanese restaurant concept. He summarized the overall goal that restaurants strive for. While the food is important, the overall feeling is paramount:

"I don't remember what I ate, but I remember how I felt."

Except for the crowd favorites like braised brisket, apricot chicken, and challah bread, I don't really remember what we ate week to week. Looking back on those moments, though, always inspires nostalgia. I realized that Shabbat and mealtime at home embodied the power of bringing people together. Aside from food, being raised in the city of Miami influenced my understanding of how hospitality can be used to create community.

Pursuing My Passion

Beaches, restaurants, and nightlife are three of the main components of Miami's famous reputation. People from around the world would travel to visit the famed nightclubs. Seeing the advertisements, the movies, and the TV shows, my friends and I always wanted to get a taste of what our city had to offer. Entrepreneurial upperclassmen at a number of high schools in the area sought to recreate "Miami-style" parties for the plebe-ians who didn't have the connections to the nightlife world. (Read: fake IDs. Shh, don't tell my mom.) Enter the "all-age ticket parties."

Venues were rented, DJs were hired, and tickets were sold for the milestone events throughout the year. Since everyone wanted to be a part of events like homecoming and prom, these after-parties became very popular and successful. I decided I was going to organize one of these events when I became a senior. Without a clue on how to pull this off, I asked my older, recently graduated friends to share their step-by-step playbook.

After drawing lots to split up the upcoming school calendar among the people interested in throwing parties, my partners and I chose graduation. Realistically, our oral agreement didn't mean anything. We knew that our event had to be legendary in order to crush any potential competitors.

Throughout the years of attending these parties, I noticed the quality began to decline significantly. As producers became profit-hungry, they started to rent cheaper locations in shadier parts of town and oversold tickets to every event. They also tried to throw parties for tag-along events like Halloween or Valentine's Day, which whittled down the overall experience. Tired of the "rinse and repeat" approach, my partners and I wanted to revive everyone's excitement. We wanted to find a high-quality venue that could truly replicate the Miami nightclub. The challenge was to find a venue that was boujie and beautiful yet wouldn't cost us a fortune. Hosting the party in South Beach was completely out of the question, since all the nightclubs are either tiny or cost a ton of money to rent. Having a bunch of high schoolers who could not purchase alcohol posed a huge opportunity cost to these clubs, forcing them to charge thousands of dollars for rent, which would prevent events from breaking even. We explored other areas around town and eventually stumbled on the perfect location in Fort Lauderdale.

During high school, I developed a deep interest in electronic dance music. Every Saturday night, I listened to the broadcast on Y100 that was streaming live from Passion Nightclub at the Hard Rock Hotel. One weekend while accompanying my friends who went to the casino there, I walked around the entertainment area and stumbled upon Passion for the first time. This was a sign I had to take action and send them an email.

A few days later, I was back at Passion, pitching my vision for our event. In the eternal moments of pause, I felt that the general manager was going to destroy the idea.

Sure! Let's go on a tour. As we walked around, I started imagining the party: seeing the bright lights, hearing the pulsing music, and dancing on the main floor with my friends. I visualized my future.

The next day, I received a disappointing phone call. Since graduation was scheduled on a Thursday, one of the busiest nights of the week for nightlife, the club would be giving up thousands of dollars in alcohol sales. If we wanted to rent the venue, we needed to buy out the venue entirely— *mucho dinero.* We were so upset, but there was nothing we could do. Business is business. The following weekend, I manifested the unexplainable.

While at my girlfriend's house eating dinner, I began to share the latest disappointment with her family. Since her parents loved partying in South Beach, I figured my project would be good table talk. I told them we were in a tough spot, since the event was scheduled for a Thursday. When her father asked me which club it was, he simply said, "I got you."

The next day, I got a phone call.

"I don't know what you did, kid, but the club is yours." Shocked, I thanked the GM and immediately got to work.

With a date and a venue locked in, we worked around the clock for the next few weeks. We were exchanging tickets and cash with promoters, posting updates online, and trying to strike deals with event sponsors. The word spread across other schools—fifteen total—which made the management of everything pretty chaotic. Pre-Venmo, Square, and Eventbrite, it was nearly impossible to keep track of it all.

The nightclub was the perfect venue for our event. It had the capacity to hold more than a thousand people. Minus a couple (all right, a crap ton) of hiccups with our guests arriving late, the club not fully opening up their space, and the police forcing us to close the doors due to curfew violations, the party was wildly successful. We created an experience that brought together hundreds of students to celebrate a pivotal milestone in their lives.

The energy from that event was addictive, and I wanted to recreate it again. But how? How could I build a career out of this? How could I build community by using food and hospitality? Can Google help me out there? Can Siri? What about Alexa? Aren't the AI gods supposed to give us the answers to all of our questions?

Meeting a Restauranteur

Unfortunately, Google's trillions of data points couldn't directly answer these types of questions at the time. One of the ways I could learn how to create a career out of a specific set of interests, though, was to ask others who seemed to have done it. Who would I ask? Nobody in my community worked in food or hospitality, at least that I knew of. Until, that is, I met a new acquaintance right in the comfort of my own home.

Harold was a friend of my French cousins who joined us one weekend when they were visiting. He was a restaurateur who owned several outposts in Paris. I had never met a restaurant owner before, and I was curious to learn more. Unfortunately, I learned this at the end of the meal, which didn't give us much time to chat. When I told him that I was traveling to Paris in a few weeks, he suggested that I come see the restaurant firsthand, where I could listen to the longer version of his story.

Weeks later, I arrived at Harold's restaurant, excited to listen to his story. After we were seated at a table covered end to end with appetizers, Harold began sharing his tale. Years ago, Harold's father opened this café, and Harold took it over when his dad retired. Harold wanted to create another concept influenced by his travels, so he opened a second and eventually a third restaurant, until he reached six. As he continued sharing, we were served different courses that represented the different chapters of the lengthy saga. Over time, his businesses enabled him to develop relationships with countless people by curating unique culinary offerings that were inspired by his global travel. This was one of the most exciting nights of my life, even more exciting than the nightclub graduation party.

I don't remember what I ate, but I [sure] remember how I felt.

That evening, I decided what I wanted to do with my life. I had no clue what it meant to own or operate a restaurant, but the stories I heard struck a chord. If restaurants could be used to generate community through food and hospitality, I would make it a priority to figure it out.

Although excited by the idea of opening a restaurant one day, I asked myself how that actually happened. What did I need to do? I wasn't on my way to culinary school to become a chef, and I didn't have a father who owned a restaurant or anyone else in my network who worked in the industry. Despite the void, I reassured myself that I had an optimistic outlook and the Law of Attraction on my side. I needed to have faith that the universe would manifest opportunities for me to transform my thoughts into things.

A week before leaving for college, I began packing my personal belongings. While going through my desk, I came across my vision board. As I was looking at it, I couldn't help but wonder if the Law of Attraction was responsible for my chance encounters during these last few years. There were a few strange coincidences I could not ignore.

Were my experiences as a basketball coach and a counselor responsible for surfacing my desire to educate others and build community? Was

Shabbat the ritual through which I developed my love for food? Was meeting Harold pure chance?

The last coincidence that really blew me away was with the nightclub. What were the odds that my girlfriend's father knew someone, who knew someone who could open up availability for the nightclub? All these coincidences were too glaring for me to ignore.

I realize that I had more opportunities than many young people. I had two happily employed, loving, and healthy parents and many relatives and family friends who were successful in one way or another. I also had a decent high school education in a safe neighborhood. I don't want to discount these privileges, but the way I see it, people are on a continuum. Some are much less privileged than me, some much more privileged. You can't change what you are born into in terms of your family, your basic characteristics, or the place you grow up. But you can make the best of whatever you start with. Using the concepts and stories discussed throughout this book as a baseline, anyone will be able to discover new opportunities for growth and advancement.

All the thoughts on my vision board became things in my life. I was admitted to the University of Florida and was able to pay for one year of living expenses with the money made from the party (no, it was not $25,000, in case you were wondering). Not only did I have a close bond with my family, but I gained an understanding of how I could use mealtime to build community. Lastly, I had discovered a new path that would enable me to use hospitality to nurture relationships with the people around me. Restaurants were calling my name. It all began with attraction.

CHAPTER TWO
Connecting the Dots with Confidence

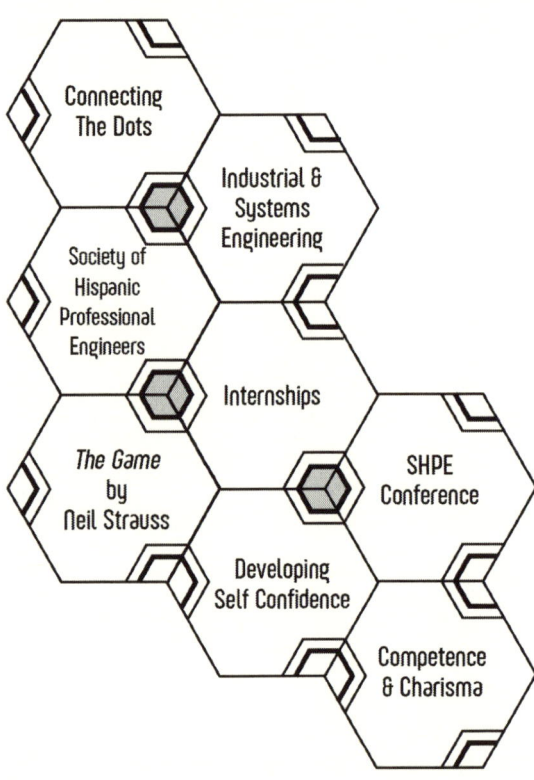

Despite my newly found direction with restaurants, I started to get very anxious about the road ahead. I was struggling with the idea that the next four years were going to be the best ones of my life. How could that be? I was confused about so many things. For starters, what did I want to study? I hadn't really thought about it, and the only conversations I had were with friends who were sold on the idea of studying business, law, or medicine—fields I was not drawn to. Next, there was the question about restaurants. How was I going to bring restaurants into my path? I wasn't heading to culinary school. Did I make a wrong decision with my university? Lastly, most of my friends that went to UF with me decided to join fraternities and sororities, while I chose to be independent from the Greek world. Being a contrarian and not following the crowd can be difficult sometimes.

It took me some time to find my stride at college. I guess that's what this stage of life was supposed to be all about—developing the confidence to find one's own way. Before filling the gaps in my external world, I started thinking how I would choose a major that suited the interests of my internal world.

Connecting the Dots

My curiosity had always driven me to ask questions to connect the dots—to try to understand how stuff works. I wondered if there was a major that taught me that.

The repetitive "what do you want to study" conversations with my friends primed me to choose to study business, which I saw as the least bad option of the trifecta that the micro-society I was a part of expected its members to pursue. While there was some degree of comfort in choosing to follow your friends—aka fitting in—something didn't feel right. There wasn't much #inspo in my life to think about other options, until another chance encounter at a Shabbat dinner.

"What are you going to study in university?" Ilan, a family friend from Israel, asked me as we enjoyed our matzah ball soup.

"I think I want to study business," I responded. Code for *I have no idea, and that is what everyone else is doing.*

"Business is learned on the job. Study engineering. It teaches you how to think."

I wondered if there was an area within engineering that would teach me how to think through connecting the dots.

Months later, I was on campus, attending welcome week. I had so many questions I wanted to ask but opted not to overwhelm my counselor. Instead, I used a crowdsourced approach and spoke with older siblings of friends I knew were at UF, upper-level students in the engineering school.

I asked them about their majors, why they chose them, and what they planned to do after school. While it was interesting to hear how they tried to bridge the gap between their interests, their choice of major, and their future plans, I was fishing for links to the restaurant world.

Although I didn't get direct answers, at least they didn't tell me I was a crazy person when I shared my desires, which was kind of a relief. (Maybe they were just being nice.) Asking my new friends about the various different majors was incredibly valuable, since it led to me discovering industrial and systems engineering.

Industrial engineers are trained to analyze systems that integrate workers, machines, materials, information, and energy to make a product or provide a service. Traditionally found in manufacturing industries, industrial engineering theory has spread to healthcare, financial services, logistics, energy, and every other industry, which has influenced universities to generalize their curriculums. Maybe this major would show me how to connect the dots within the restaurant world.

With some direction on how to begin my educational journey, it was time to make some friends.

Setting Goals for Tomorrow

Attending in-state university has its pros and cons. On one hand, there might be numerous people from your hometown joining you on the journey to school. On the other, these same wonderful humans are on the journey right alongside you. In other words, it's easy to get comfortable in your bubble. I had plenty of friends who went to UF, but almost all of them immediately chose to join the fraternity and sorority community, which required them to give up nearly all of their free time, leaving me friendless. Choosing not to follow the tide, I wasn't sure where to begin on my quest to find new amigos.

Most of my engineering colleagues were either shy and didn't open up or felt pressured to continuously study for class. I remember one of the tricks I used to make new friends when I transferred to a new high school: getting involved.

Colleges have thousands of student organizations that bring people together for all sorts of causes and interests. These interests ranged far beyond the typical high school student groups. I started noticing the flyers on the different bulletin boards around campus: outdoor tightrope, tai chi, solar-powered drone racing, skydiving club, outdoor adventures, etc. The list was endless. While I was open to meeting new, diverse people, I still wanted to interact with those who shared the same values as I did.

One day, while waiting for the elevator in my dorm building, I noticed the words "HISPANIC ENGINEER" posted on the announcements board. Taking a closer look, I scanned the flyer, which was promoting the first meeting for the Society of Hispanic Professional Engineers (SHPE) next week. On the bottom was written: "Free *Arroz con Pollo—chicken and rice—* will be served." My foodie senses were tingling.

While free food was a major component of the SHPE organization's overwhelming success in retaining their member base, there were plenty of other programs that the organization offered to inspire the two-hundred-plus *Venezolanos, Colombianos, Argentinos, Peruanos*, and many more to return meeting after meeting.

At the first meeting, I served myself some arroz con pollo, topped it off with pink sauce (the quintessential Latin condiment), grabbed a seat next to someone new, and tried striking up a conversation. A few minutes later, the lights dimmed, and the words "**$1000 GFT SCHOLARSHIP**" appeared in big, bold letters in the front of the room. The room went silent, and the meeting began.

The Goals for Tomorrow (GFT) Scholarship was an award given to three students who "exhibited future leadership potential," whatever that meant. Although the application would be due toward the end of the semester, the intent was to inspire new members to get involved early on. Maybe I would volunteer some of my time here, make new friends, eat arroz con pollo, and earn some cash while doing so.

The next topic presented was the SHPE Conference, which was a weekend job fair attended by hundreds of companies aiming to hire thousands of students for full-time jobs and summer internships. Since SHPE-UF had corporate partners that sponsored chapter development activities, we were able to maintain a strong presence at the conference. Getting paid for trying to get an internship or a job? Seemed like a win-win situation.

Following my visionary practices, I printed out a picture of the SHPE logo and put it above my desk in my dorm room, next to the pictures of my family. Every month, I attended meetings and volunteered time working with the VP of corporate affairs. I was interested in fundraising and developing relationships with companies. Through my activities, I made a new group of friends, some of whom even shared class with me. At least I now had a couple of amigos to enjoy arroz con pollo and study with.

At the end of the semester, I was selected as one of the three winners for the GFT award. As a recipient, I was responsible for organizing a soccer tournament, which raised the funds for the following year's scholarship. Since I was already working with the VP of corporate, my main responsibility was to raise funds from our partner organizations. After weeks of planning and preparation, we managed to register twenty-five teams and raise six thousand dollars. I realized that I loved the relationship-building and fundraising tasks of the VP corporate and volunteered in that position for the upcoming year.

I couldn't identify whether it was the Hispanic or the community builder in me that was so drawn to this organization. I started to realize how these organizations could be used as stepping-stones toward career opportunities. They give us the chance to get our hands dirty by launching projects and building relationships with others while generating profits for causes we believe in. All of these skills attract organizations when they are identifying their next new hire.

Free food is always a motivation for college students to attend meetings. However, I believe that the mindset of setting goals for tomorrow that our SHPE culture instilled was the number one reason for our engagement. We were able to develop our professional identities alongside one another and have fun doing it. It was awesome to have a group of friends who worked hard and celebrated our eventual successes when we began landing our first jobs.

Internships

Before signing the contract for your first full time job, it might be wise to get a few "practice" rounds in. Internships provide a glimpse into the real-world experience of being on the job within a specific vocation. While the day-to-day might seem monotonous and unexciting, we learn what it means to have a job, which includes: business etiquette (promptness, neatness, courtesy, learning to respect the hierarchy), communicating with colleagues, becoming exposed to an industry and what it means to be a part of something bigger—a large company, in my case. If getting experience isn't enough of a selling point, internships can be paid or applied as school credit. Internships are an investment in figuring out in what direction we want to take our careers.

My favorite aspect of serving as the VP of corporate affairs for SHPE was that I had the ability to use the power of hospitality to create connections between our members and company recruiters. The SHPE barbecue was the premier networking event that the VP corporate was in charge of organizing. Every year, we catered a fully loaded barbecue buffet so that members and recruiters could grab a bite to eat and develop a relationship over a quality meal. This took place outside of the career fair that always created a chaotic environment for everyone in attendance. Organizing these events is what helped me flex my public relations muscles. I began to practice what my mom had been teaching me over the years.

An hour before my first SHPE barbecue was set to open, I asked one of the recruiters for advice on getting a job in finance. *I still didn't have any possibilities that bridged the gap between engineering and restaurants, so I opted to explore options within reach.* He told me he had some colleagues he could introduce me to. What he didn't tell me, though, was that those colleagues were a part of his own organization. Thinking I was on the finance internship track, I enthusiastically shared my stories during the behavioral interview I had the next morning. A few weeks later, I received an offer to join the operations division of General Electric in Erie, Pennsylvania. Was I really going to turn this down because it wasn't *exactly* what I wanted? No. That would be too millennial of me.

That summer, I was assigned to work with the quality assurance team. Our responsibility was to measure the quality of the locomotives we were manufacturing within our complex supply chain. That's a fancy way of saying we tracked the mistakes made across the different processes. My tasks as an intern involved producing summarized reports for the leadership team and following up with the owners of the different Correction Action Requests. I wouldn't say it was a particularly exhilarating experience. Alas, it was interesting to be exposed to the inner workings of a multibillion-dollar corporation that had been around for one-hundred-plus years. I was fascinated by the ability our small team had to connect the dots across the large organization. Ten weeks later, I was on my way back to campus, reflecting on what I had lived through and what I wanted out of my next internship the following summer.

I was always attracted to the energy of New York City. In hopes of landing an internship in the city, I added a picture of the Empire State Building to my vision board. Whenever I stared at it, I was reminded of the dynamic experiences of visiting my family there. I wanted to attract that into my life.

It isn't necessarily smooth sailing for systems engineers who want to intern in New York, since there aren't many companies there that hire people in my major. Systems engineers are usually hired by companies in the manufacturing, agriculture, healthcare, or logistics industries, which tend to be located in rural areas. Asking the upper-level students for some advice on how to get to New York, they advised me that investment banks hired systems engineers in their operations division, but they never came to recruit at our career fair. How would I get to these investment banks? They recruited almost exclusively from the Ivy Leagues. My backdoor would be at the upcoming SHPE Conference in Anaheim, California.

Part of what makes college the best years of our lives are the spontaneous adventures we sprinkle throughout the journey. Although it might seem like I was a robot who studied and volunteered all my time while in college, I still had the electronic dance music Miami boy in me. Even though I was focused on getting a banking internship at the SHPE Conference, Avicii (a very famous DJ) was scheduled to be in town the night before the conference began. In life, we choose to take risks and live with the consequences of our decisions. In this case, enjoy an epic concert by one of the most popular DJs, followed by an exhausting sleepless flight across the country, prior to arguably one of the most pivotal moments of my college career to date.

Landing in California, I took a taxi to the hotel, checked into my room, took a freezing-cold shower, suited up, chugged coffee, and made my way down to the conference. I entered the workshop of PJ Malcolm, a global investment bank headquartered in New York. I pinpointed the recruiter at the front of the room, walked right up to introduce myself, and stretched out my hand with confidence. She beat me to it.

"Hi, I'm Rebecca!"

"Hi, Rebecca, I'm Errrrrrrrrrrnesto," I replied with a huge grin across my face. (Not your typical way to introduce yourself to a corporate recruiter.)

"Hey, that's not fair! I can't roll my R's like that! Asians can't do that!" She smiled.

"Well, we're just not gonna get along then." I crossed my arms and turned away.

She laughed. I laughed. It was awesome. All guard was dropped.

Following a few more exchanges, Rebecca introduced me to the recruiter in the operations division of the company. We spoke about what I was looking for and set up a time to continue the discussion the next morning.

Weeks later, after accepting my internship, I got a call from someone asking for an "Errrrrnesto." It was Rebecca—who had significantly improved her r-rolling. Sometimes, being weird makes you memorable.

Although I was sleep deprived, exhausted, and laughed about everything while I was interacting with Rebecca, I wasn't always as bold with my remarks—especially in these kinds of *stressful* situations. Actually, when it came to establishing emotional connections with strangers— female strangers—I had to deal with major anxiety attacks that would arise due to irrational fears I had developed during my teenage years.

Picking Myself Up

Years before watching *The Secret* with my dad, I learned about the Law of Attraction by experiencing its ugly side. At the onset of my teenage years, I started to develop an irrational fear of interacting with women. This was probably caused by some sort of childhood trauma or insecurity about my weight—I'm not quite sure, to be honest. What I did notice is that while all my friends started to hit puberty and chase girls, I created distractions to avoid interacting with them entirely. At dance parties on the weekends, my guy friends fearlessly danced with the girls, while I opted to play games on my crappy Nokia phone in the corner of the room, fearing any social contact with them. I was manifesting my reality in the worst of ways, long before I even realized what I was doing. One night, an angel appeared, giving me the jolt to change my perspective.

"Come on, Ernie, let's dance!" Natalie grabbed my hand and dragged me out onto the dance floor. She put my arms around her waist and put hers on my shoulder for my first slow dance. I must have looked pretty goofy. Being a full head taller than she and everyone else in my grade made it an awkward moment, or so I thought. This was the shock I needed that began my social transformation.

After that night, I started opening up and eventually developed crushes on a few of the ladies in my grade. Whenever I worked up the courage to ask one out on a date, I was rejected and reminded that we were just friends. Looking around my friend circles, all the guys were either going out or making out with their significant other as I kept getting placed in this mysterious "friend zone." *Why me?* As this continued to happen, my relationship to the idea of sexual attraction started becoming muddled.

If only all those parents knew how I really felt when they teased me about the horde of girls who were chasing me. There were no screaming fans. Just rejection after rejection. Reflecting on some of the root causes, the conclusion I came to was that I never developed the flirting skills that my guy friends learned at sleepaway camp while I continued to attend sports camps every summer, free of contact with females. Whether that was true or not didn't matter, because whatever was in my head was being reflected in reality. Thoughts became things.

I kept telling myself that when I went to college, I'd learn how to flirt with women—what I always thought I wanted. But how could I learn those things? Although Google couldn't guide me on combining restaurants and systems engineering, it was much better at giving dating advice. Through my searches, I stumbled upon *The Game*, a book written by Neil Strauss, which introduced me to the world of pick-up artists.

During my first two years of college, I dedicated my weekend time diving into the game, implementing the tips and tricks whenever I went out with my friends. In the spring semester of my freshman year, I changed my position on frat life and decided to join one with friends I had made in my dorms. Aside from meeting an intelligent group of dudes who weren't as "bro-y" as most frat culture depicted, joining the fraternity was a great decision because it put me in situations where I could apply the lessons I had learned on how to attract women.

Spoiler alert: at the conclusion of *The Game*, the author realizes that the point of pick-up isn't about getting with as many women as possible, but rather about developing the confidence within to pursue what you want in life, whether that be relationships, philanthropy, entrepreneurial endeavors, etc. The book chronicles the "exciting" stories of casual sex and one-night stands, but those didn't really jibe with me. I never wanted to become a shady pick-up artist; I simply wanted to learn how to overcome my insecurities and develop the confidence to attract the women that I was fascinated by.

When I first started living in the fraternity house, surrounded by women, alcohol, and social events, my insecurities would arise, causing me to recede back to my thirteen-year-old self, hiding behind my Nokia. No matter how debilitating those flashbacks were, I needed to break through the resistance and face my fears head-on. Eventually, I started dating someone, and my exercises shifted toward recognizing my accomplishments to improve my self-confidence.

I realized that my insecurities didn't stem from not knowing the right way to open with a joke or how to approach a group of women. Rather, they were from a lack of confidence in expressing who I was, what I had accomplished, and where I was headed—similar to the major takeaway from *The Game*. This conclusion was solidified for me weeks after returning from my internship experience in Erie, Pennsylvania.

Going into that summer, I declared an intention to lose twenty-five pounds, since I had gained extra weight from my poor eating and drinking habits while living in the fraternity house. I cut out a picture of someone with a six-pack from *Men's Health* magazine and put it up on my vision board. While I was in Erie, I adopted a weekly practice where I planned my activities, which included working out, cooking nutritious food, and going out with new intern friends.

Using the P90X fitness plan, I lost twenty pounds and reshaped my understanding of how mindset impacted reality. My self-confidence had shot through the roof, which flooded into other areas of my life. Coming back from that summer experience with a refreshed perspective, I felt more confident than ever that I would figure out how to achieve whatever I put my mind to. I was heading to New York City, creating the intention of bringing restaurants into my reality.

While a small voice in my head was nagging me about the fact that I wasn't learning how to cook or set a table, I reminded myself that I had made leaps and bounds developing self-confidence, building a social network of friends and classmates, and learning about systems engineering theory. Most books about success highlight the importance of confidence and networking. What they don't do is tell you how to fix whatever your specific individual issues are. You have to figure that out for yourself. It may take more time than you think it should, and others may not notice your accomplishments. You may not get any kudos, and that's okay. Not everything in life is a double-tap heart or a digital thumbs-up. You can give them to yourself, acknowledging the progress you've made resulting from the actions you've taken. Everyone is a NewBee, living through their unique journey and experiences.

At the beginning of school, agonizing over the questions in my head was not helpful. I needed to get out there and explore the college world. Cross-pollinating through different student organizations, social groups, companies, and conferences, I began to develop an unshakable confidence in myself, despite not having the answers at the ready. Following these first years of college, my experiences enabled me to develop the confidence, the competence, and the charisma required to create a product that would tease me with the possibility of bridging the worlds of hospitality and systems engineering.

CHAPTER THREE
Creating My Mystique

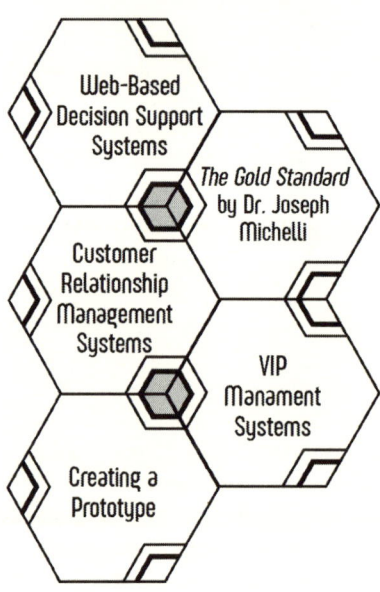

Web-Based Decision Support Systems

The Gold Standard by Dr. Joseph Michelli

Customer Relationship Management Systems

VIP Manament Systems

Creating a Prototype

A significant component of the college/university experience is the choice of a major, a collection of about thirty-two courses within an area of study. While a majority of them are already chosen for you as requirements, there is room to explore personal interests through taking classes that are on a list of electives. I'm going to assume that within your major, there are a couple of courses with your name on them—topics that you are fascinated by and wish to learn more about. Depending on your field of interest, these courses will teach you the skills to create a product or a service for the world, be it a detailed essay or report, a complex spreadsheet model or statistics experiment, a perfectly captured photo, a public speech, or how to produce an event. Searching for ways to transform my upcoming internship into a fulfilling experience, I reflected on how I could directly apply what I learned in my favorite classes into the real world.

Database Programming was that course for me. It taught me how to design websites that displayed data to support decision-making in companies. We built software programs that gave management teams visibility into the key performance indicators (KPIs) that displayed different statistics of the business, which might include: the number of widgets sold, the total hours of labor required to create those products, or the percentage of sales that were returned. I gave 120 percent effort, devouring the content, attending office hours, and collaborating with other students to finish the group assignments. I wondered if there was a way I could apply the lessons learned from class into the restaurant business.

The Ritz-Carlton Mystique

At the end of my junior year, I was on my way to New York City for my internship in the banking world. New York City summers generate an energy that is difficult to describe. The restaurants, the parks, the Broadway shows, the happy hours—the list goes on. It's safe to say that that are tons of distractions to be had with your friends. I wanted to do it all, but I had to make a decision. Was I going to gallivant around the city or focus on finding a way to merge systems engineering with hospitality? Choosing the latter, I thought about how I could apply what I had learned from a book I had read about one of the leading hotel companies in the world, the Ritz-Carlton.

The Ritz-Carlton developed a unique training program that is responsible for the five-star service received at any property around the world. At any touchpoint of the guest experience, whether it's checking in at the lobby, dining on-property, sipping poolside beverages, or enjoying a massage at the spa, every employee has access to data on each guest. The private, sensitive data is hidden from sight. Yet, key details like special dates, allergies, favorite foods, special interests, and guest preferences are displayed to staff. If they see an opportunity to make a moment memorable, they are empowered and trained to do so, greatly enhancing the guest experience. I thought of how I could apply this to other sectors of the hospitality business. Just before leaving for New York, I shared my findings with my mom's colleagues.

My mom works for a corporate travel agency that serves international luxury brands and private leisure clients. In order to recommend unforgettable experiences, her agency has had to develop relationships with the elite hotels and restaurants in the cities where her clients travel. Thinking about the Ritz-Carlton's technology, I asked Doris, the owner of the agency, how they kept track of their clients' travel and dining preferences in order to enhance recommendations when they travel.

"Well, we just remember!" she explained, pointing to her head and giving me a wink.

There is no way that is possible when you are catering to hundreds, if not thousands, of clients. I remember thinking that all the data could be stored in the kind of database that I had just learned how to build and analyze.

Creating "mystique" isn't only a value taught to every employee of the Ritz-Carlton, it's also the name of the powerful customer relationship management (CRM) system that supports the delivery of that value. The Oxford English dictionary defines Mystique is as "a fascinating aura of mystery, awe, and power surrounding someone or something." The Ritz-Carlton's attention to detail with every guest interaction is what led to their reputation as one of the leading hospitality organizations in the world. I started to wonder how the restaurant business could benefit from access to this type of information on their guests. Could restaurants serve their guests with the attention that each of their unique needs requires? Could they create their own mystique?

Creating Mystique for Nightclubs

While talking with Doris, I asked her if she had contacts in the New York City hospitality scene with whom I could share my technology ideas. After exchanging a few emails, I was connected with one of the hottest night-clubs in the Meatpacking District. I set up time to meet with Mike, the marketing director, when I moved into town a few weeks later.

"So, what do you want, kid?" the marketing director asked as he skeptically glanced through my résumé.

"I'm a systems engineer who wants to create a system to help your club keep track of its guests."

Mike raised an eyebrow and responded, "Tell me more."

A CRM system centralizes information collected from customers in order to personalize how they are marketed and sold to. The goal of hospitality businesses—really, any business—should be to build exceptional relationships with guests by understanding their needs and surpassing their expectations. Why wouldn't every restaurant or nightclub use a system like Mystique?

Nightclubs and entertainment venues have historically grown by partnering with promoters. Businesses hire and motivate socialites to attract their networks of hundreds (sometimes thousands) of people who enjoy spending their time and money in nightclubs and restaurants. Although nightclubs do realize the sales from the people brought in through this model, the key information about their end user—the guests they serve—is "owned" by the promoters. These promoters can hold businesses hostage and threaten to take their clients elsewhere if their demands aren't met. Fortunately, technology can be used to prevent these conflicts and help nightclubs form relationships directly with each guest.

Breaking that long pause, I asked him how the club kept track of their VIP members. I guess he was interested because he immediately jumped into explaining their process: how guests lined up outside, who checked them in, where they went, etc. Within twenty minutes, I had received a high-level explanation of the VIP customer lifecycle. He continued.

"And this paper is where everything is stored." He took out a form that had guest information, what they ordered, what table they sat at, and who served them.

Time slowed down. I was hung up on this eight-by-eleven sheet of paper. How is it possible that a nightclub that brought in hundreds of thousands of dollars was using an old-school pen to keep track of this crucial data? Why wasn't I holding an iPad?

"At the end of the night, the server asks the guest to sign *the paper,* and their credit card, receipt, and ID are returned. The next day, an intern enters it into our program."

Oh, a program? I needed to pry.

I immediately knew that the use of paper was a missed opportunity to simplify collecting the data and reduce errors from manual entry. Hard to imagine zero mistakes getting a form signed in the middle of a loud, raging nightclub with champagne flying everywhere at four in the morning. It definitely is a time-suck to key in the information on each of these forms every damn day. I felt like everything should have been handled with a quick swipe, sign, and tap.

When I asked him about the program, he showed me an archaic-looking application that someone had developed a few months earlier. Since I was taking courses in data analysis, I asked if it was possible to export the data into Excel. Having that ability would allow the nightclub to analyze what products were ordered, which employees sold the most, and which nights were the most popular, with a couple of keystrokes and mouse clicks. Since the program could not export the data, I thought of building something similar to what I had built in my database-programming class.

"I'm going to build you something that will eliminate the use of paper and simplify the capture of this information. We can then look at how we can use this information to personalize the experience for your guests," I proposed to Mike.

Mike was curious to see what I had in mind and agreed that we would meet every couple of weeks to review my progress.

Educated Guesses

Despite not knowing exactly what I was going to do, I knew I had to take advantage of the opportunity in front of me. It was up to me to figure out how to use the knowledge I had, create a few assumptions, and take an educated guess.

I started with the resources I had available: my course notes, homework assignments, and final project document. I began reviewing how I could adapt these for a nightclub. The different objects that my technology needed to track were guests, the products they ordered, the employees who sold the products, the date of all the events, and the transactions that brought everything together. After drafting a project outline, I mocked up three webpages on my notepad to convey to the team what I would start working on. Mike confirmed this was a suitable starting point.

After eight weeks of coding and testing, I demonstrated to Mike and a few other managers how my tool could be used to track guests, product sales, and employees. When I finished, the team seemed pleased, as they asked several follow-up questions. Although my tool had basic functionality, I knew it had its drawbacks and needed a more significant investment. It was a minimum viable product, after all.

Before walking out, I tried convincing the team to give me a $1,500 budget to build the next iteration of the tool—a demo that could work in a live environment. I was spitballing numbers and thought it was a solid estimate. After a couple of weeks, though, I received a rejection email, which was a total burn. To be honest, I really didn't have a plan. So, it was probably for the best. I did get something out of it, though.

Seeing the smiles and experiencing the engagement from the team generated an emotion that felt even better than completing the database course just a few months prior. This project was the intersection I had been looking for since starting college! The nexus of systems engineering and hospitality existed, and I had just lived and breathed it for the past ten weeks. How could I chase more of these types of experiences?

Applying something learned in the classroom to the real world can have surprising effects. If you ask a bunch of friends to take their headshots and use photo-editing software to make them professional, you might discover your passion for getting involved in media production or client service work. Perhaps there are businesses in your city that are in need of someone to come in and help them analyze some of their numbers or conduct cold calls to build sales. Alchemizing the lessons learned from a classroom into the real world will result in insights that enable you to discover the next steps you can take in your journey.

After that summer, I decided I would shift my north star. I wanted to start focusing on the idea of developing technology for restaurants to enhance the guest experience. Just a few weeks after returning to school, I discovered there was an entire profession solely dedicated to the very goal of creating technology to enhance the customer experience—one that creates technology platforms exactly like Mystique.

CHAPTER FOUR
Press Yourself

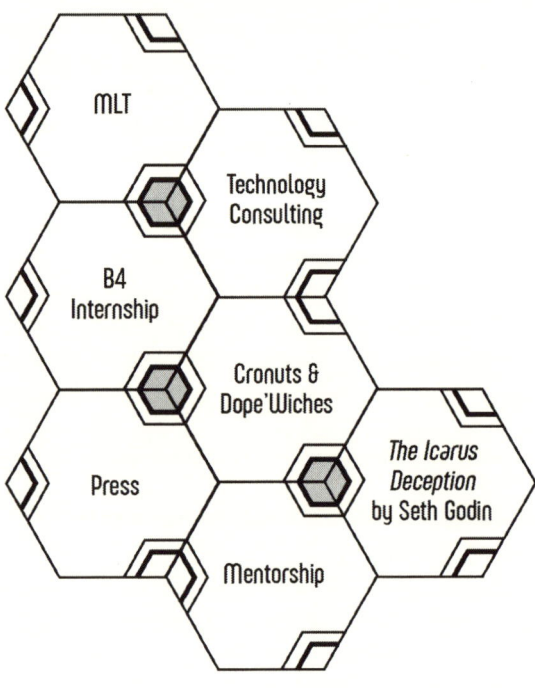

Toward the end of my college experience, I needed to start thinking about the dreaded job search. I wanted to see how I could weave my interests into my first full-time gig. To learn more about how to do this, I applied to join MLT, a professional development organization that champions diversity and inclusion hiring across Fortune 500 companies. Going through the Career Prep program led to my next internship within the technology consulting world. After returning to campus for my senior year, I started my first food company, Press, whose underlying ethos and motto represented the grind required to create one's own path, despite not having all the answers.

Diverse Interests, Diverse Organizations

In my junior year of college, I applied to Management Leadership 4 Tomorrow (MLT), a professional development program that helped students of Hispanic and African American origin prepare for jobs in the corporate world. David, one of my childhood friends, had referred me to the organization, even though I had not maintained an active relationship with him. I always respected his ability to use the available resources to chart his own path and felt that if I put myself in similar environments to his, I could meet people who would lead me toward creating my own projects.

MLT trains people across the spectrum of career stages to discover professional opportunities in line with their interests and skills. They partner with organizations such as Goldman Sachs, Vanguard, Pepsi, Deloitte, and several others to attract a diverse talent pool beginning careers in finance, social impact, law, engineering, technology, etc. As a participant of the Career Prep program, I was paired with a career coach who had years of experience preparing students for the job search. These coaches pushed students beyond their comfort zones to help them discover jobs and career opportunities that they didn't realize existed. My coach started pushing me on our first five-minute conversation.

That call was at eight o'clock Friday morning, after a long night with friends at the bar.

"Good morning, Ernesto. Why don't we start with you telling me a little about yourself." I felt Coach A, my coach, was speaking to me with extreme passive aggression. Or maybe it was just the hangover.

I had been practicing my spiel over and over with recruiters at prior career fairs, internships, and interviews. Forty-five seconds into my pitch, I was hit with, "You seem like a Type B, Ernesto, almost like you don't care."

Was I boring?

Stunned, I didn't know how to move forward. She apologized for the interruption and asked if I had anything else to add.

"I created a guest-tracking technology product for a nightclub this past summer."

"Oh? And what was that like?" she inquired.

As I began recounting my former side hustle, I felt a jolt of energy that eradicated the hangover and enabled me to launch into a more passionate story. When I finished, Coach A asked if I had ever considered technology consulting. I'd never heard of it.

"That's what you did this summer. You should look into it as part of our first assignment."

In the first few weeks of the program, we completed assignments that included crafting our résumés and cover letters, reading about case studies, and researching companies. Coach A pushed me to think about how I could combine what the hospitality and the consulting companies offered in terms of internships. She told me that it would be helpful to the recruiters if they could draw a line between my experiences and what their companies were looking for in candidates. Reflecting on our conversations, I can't help but wonder if Coach A was trying to teach me about cross-pollination years before I even realized what it was.

Because of the way the program was structured, we would have multiple chances to meet with these recruiters and share our stories. MLT invested heavily in networking opportunities for participants to get together a few times throughout the year to meet the partner organizations. At the first seminar, I interacted with recruiters and alumni from the partner companies. Returning from that seminar, I printed pictures of the logos of companies in the tech consulting space and added them to my vision board. Now, it was time to focus on GTO— "get the offer—MLT's "warrior chant" for receiving an internship or full-time offer.

While the first seminar was more of a meet and greet, the second seminar was dedicated to the interview process, one of the most daunting aspects of the internship search. Aside from the education workshops, there were specific time slots that were set aside for partner organizations to interview candidates. Prior to the weekend, the partner companies arranged phone interviews so that they could use the in-person time for final-round interviews. One of the companies that I had talked with offered me a time slot during that seminar. The partner I interviewed with wanted to talk trash the entire time. As someone who works in the waste-management industry, he asked me about how technology could be used to simplify business operations. Strange yet interesting topic. He told me that I would hear back in a couple of weeks.

If it were not for the preparation that MLT provided, I would not have been prepared to go through the rigorous process of discovering all the different career paths that became available to me. Joining a program like this can help anyone find new approaches for their career. Joining *any* program that exposes you to professionals in one of your fields of interest—professionals who have signaled their willingness to help by getting involved in such a program—will teach you valuable lessons. They won't be the same as mine, and they may not be as immediately helpful. But your world will open up as you venture into programs like these.

Late December, I received my Hanukkah gift, an offer to work at Big4 (B4), a global consulting corporation! Since the job would be in New York City, and I was genuinely excited, I decided to accept it so that I could get back to my regularly scheduled (collegiate) programming.

The Next Cronut?

The internship with B4 gave me a taste of the life of an analyst in the con-sulting world. Although I traveled every week, I had tons of flexibility and freedom to work on my own projects during off-hours. I dedicate the next chapter to the experience with B4 as a full-timer. For now, I want to share how that flexibility enabled me to create my first food company.

In 2013, Dominique Ansel, one of New York City's most revered pastry chefs, announced the birth of the Cronut. Part donut, part croissant, the flaky pastry was offered to a small group of people, one of whom wrote a piece for *New York Magazine*. By the Cronut's third day on sale, over one hundred fans lined up outside of Ansel's SoHo bakery in the morning, anxiously waiting for a taste of the rumored treat.

With each passing day, the demand grew stronger, and people were arriving earlier and earlier to beat the rush. With the burgeoning hype, people started to resell the treats for up to twenty times the price. Bakeries around the world tried to launch their own versions. I was amazed by this. *How the hell can I do that? What two things could I combine to create hype like this?* I reminisced about my first love: ice cream.

Growing up, making ice cream sundaes was part of my regular routine. I'm not talking about a scoop or two of ice cream. Rather, fully loaded productions with Oreo cookies, maraschino cherries, chocolate fudge, whipped cream, all topped with milk so that I could mix it together and drink it out of the plastic straw that came attached to the bowl—the bowls that every kid from the 90s grew up eating out of. I had a great time until my grandma took me to a doctor who placed a moratorium on these decadent desserts. At the time, it felt like my life was over. I grew out of that feeling (and out of my clothes), shot up a couple of inches, and returned to a more normal weight/height ratio. I didn't know it at the time, but ice cream would creep back into my life in a way I never imagined.

One day, while running around Central Park, the ice cream gods sent a bolt of lightning to jolt me with #inspo. Ice cream and donuts. Hot and Cold. Panini-pressed ice-cream donut sandwiches!

When I shared the revelation with my friends, they all said it was impossible, and that it would melt. However, they reassured me that they would definitely be there for the taste test if I could make it work. Duh...

To start experimenting, I bought some kitchen tools, a few pints of ice cream, and two dozen donuts. Despite multiple failures with different types of pans, I was determined to make it work. Iterating my approach, I froze the sandwich pre-sear in order to prevent it from melting. That sort of worked until I had to flip the sandwich to sear the other side. I needed something easier. Looking around the apartment, I noticed a dusty George Foreman grill on the top shelf of the closet. Ah ha—this was it! Grill the sandwich from both ends at the same time. The "Dope'Wich" was born.

The fluffy, hot and cold, panini-pressed ice cream donut sandwich made its debut at a dinner party with my friends in the city that summer. No, they did not melt. Yes, it was incredibly decadent and delicious. I remember thinking to myself: *Could the Dope'Wich become the next Cronut?*

Press Yourself

"Getting started" is different for every entrepreneur. Some might advise testing to discover whether there is demand for the product before investing the time to create it. Steve Jobs would have said that customers don't know what they want until you give it to them. Either option might be correct, depending on the product. Since I had already completed both the product development and the market testing phases, I moved on to creating an identity.

"Press" would be the name of the company to represent the way which we prepared our products—using a blistering-hot panini press—and also to reflect the approach that we applied to bettering our lives. "Press Yourself" became our motto. By reading books, listening to podcasts, learning skills, and developing positive habits, we strive for improvement. Personal development is foundational to cross-pollination.

Press expanded the frontier of desserts by combining different ingredients with distinct physical properties to create innovative products. I wanted to share my message with the world. So, I rushed to purchase a bunch of website domains, started a few logo contests on 99designs, registered my business online, and blocked off a bunch of social media pages, spending hundreds of dollars on the business without a single sale.

The fraternity was Press's first customers. At our first weekly meeting, I announced that I would be selling Dope'Wiches after the next social event for $4 a pop, first come, first serve.

Leading up to the event, I prepared thirty-six Dope'Wiches at home and stored them in my freezer. I drafted a list of items that I needed to bring with me to the frat house for a proper setup. Without having lived through an actual event, it was nearly impossible for me to predict all the little details that were needed to pull this off successfully. I was definitely unprepared, but my friends were patient and forgiving. In the hour leading up to my first opening—at 2 a.m.—I was getting nervous and thought that I was going to mess everything up somehow. Maybe I was just being hard on myself—typical human behavior that often sabotages success.

The moment I placed the first Dope'Wich on the grill and the searing pans began caramelizing the sugars to create the smell of crème brulée, everyone started cheering, and my worries melted away. Three dozen Dope'Wiches later, I was out of stock, and the debut had come to an end. While the sizzle faded, I reflected on how to improve delivery of the service. I needed to keep practicing.

Over the next few weeks, I used the fraternity as a platform to sell Dope'Wiches at socials and game-day barbecues. Each of these events allowed me to continue improving the cutting, storing, transporting, and preparing of the product. I was the systems engineer for Press. One day, I was sharing my adventures with my mentor and close friend, Professor Whitney, who would challenge me at my own game.

I met "Whit" just after completing the nightclub project. He was curious about student entrepreneurs. When I told him about my early trials with the Dope'Wich, he challenged me to serve one hundred Dope'Wiches to a crowd of entrepreneurs at the next Startup Weekend event downtown.

"Press Yourself," he said as I was walking out of the office.

I couldn't even fit that many in my freezer!

Startup Weekend is a seventy-two-hour competition where entrepreneurs present their prototypes to a panel of judges, in hopes of winning seed funding to actually build their product. These events are usually attended by members of the local entrepreneurial community, including founders, the media, and investors. Feeding the movers and shakers of Gainesville could launch Press into the spotlight.

Without a freezer that could hold the hundred Dope'Wiches, I had to get creative. Shout out to the scientists who invented dry ice, and YouTube for teaching me how to create a makeshift freezer with a cooler.

With the help of my brother, I was able to make the hundred Dope'Wiches in under two hours, place them in the "freezer," and grab everything else we needed. We packed the car and drove to the competition. While we were setting up, the photographer came over and inquired about what we were doing. I told him to return in ten minutes, ready to capture the moment.

The sear, sizzle, and smell of a Dope'Wich being pressed had a serious crowd-building ability. Whit was a friend of the Startup Weekend organization and let them know that I was providing a light bite before the competition began. The crowd started to build up around our table as we started juggling the preparation, presentation, and service of eight Dope'Wiches simultaneously. The photographer was able to capture memorable first-bite reactions. Everyone asked me how to get Press at their next event. I told them to message me through Facebook. Not having business cards was a serious newbie mistake—another item I needed to add to my master checklist. After burning through our inventory, the audience took their seats, and the competition began. One-hundred-person Dope'Wich event. Check.

I was lucky to have someone like Whit on my team who pushed me to press myself. It's mentors like this who are responsible for providing wisdom, guidance, and the chance for us to further our lives. But how do you find a mentor in your specific field who is willing to help you out? There isn't a one-size-fits-all approach to this, but here's how I found some of mine.

Mentorship

While registering for coursework, my advisor recommended that I go across the hall and meet Professor Whit, one of the College of Engineering's faculty dedicated to the entrepreneurial world. I was excited to meet someone who could help me find the doors to open to discover new opportunities, especially those that fit my passion for entrepreneurship in the hospitality space. After challenging me with the hundred-person event, Whit and I continued to chat about incorporating entrepreneurship principles into careers. He eventually invited me to sign up for his course on innovation theories in the engineering world.

Professor Whitney's class was popular and attracted a diverse group of engineers. I enrolled, intrigued by the curriculum and the energy he would bring to the classroom. There was an added bonus of learning from guest lecturers. Every week, businesspeople from the Gainesville community would share their stories with our class, which complemented the lesson of the week. Halfway through the semester, we had the special opportunity to meet with John, a management consultant who spent 80 percent of his time on the road traveling for business.

John is a subject matter expert on a variety of topics in the business world, including leadership, strategy, talent management, organizational development, and more. Put simply, he has become an expert in business by reading over one hundred books a year, for the past twenty years, that span all areas of business excellence. He began this practice when he was in his twenties. His boss would give him a book on Monday and expect to discuss it on Friday over lunch. Reading so many stories of success, failure, and strategic approaches for the past two decades has enabled him to coach executive teams at Fortune 500 corporations. Why was he in the class with us, a bunch of seniors? John came to guide the future generation of leaders on how hard work, passion, and the right combination of mentors all contribute to success.

During these weekly sessions, the students were given little slips of paper that we used to ask the speaker questions. With John continuing to reiterate the importance of building a team of support players, it was only natural that one of the slips of paper included the question: "How can we get you as a mentor?"

Every year, John offered the students the same challenge that he was offered in his twenties: read and summarize three books and be prepared to discuss them over a meal. I needed to complete this challenge to see if John had *any* insight on how I could continue to chase the intersection of hospitality, systems engineering, and technology. With my time split between attending class, pressing sandwiches, and hanging out with friends, I definitely could make room to form a disciplined reading habit.

After I submitted my responses, John agreed to meet for lunch. When I told John about my interests in hospitality and technology and my plans of going into consulting, his eyes lit up. In an instant, he started sharing his excitement about the power of hospitality and rattled off the titles of three more books that I absolutely needed to read. He reiterated the importance of building relationships with mentors. I asked him how one did that, and he said it was simple. The first step is to identify something you want to learn about or get involved with. The next step involves reaching out to people who work in that field, sharing that curiosity with them, and asking how you could learn more. Offering your perspective or time to assist them in completing a task is a way of demonstrating your commitment to the process.

The person might realize that you are worth their investment of time. You may be given a chance to join a team or be presented with another probationary challenge. This mutual exchange of value makes the experience worthwhile. I didn't exactly understand what that exchange entailed, but I would find out soon enough when I would have to develop relationships in the corporate world. At the end of our meal, I thanked John for his time and his wisdom.

"Keeping in touch … is the key to maintaining your relationships in your network," he said.

More of that public relations advice my mom taught me.

Pressing Pause

With a few weeks left until graduation, I started to wind down and prepare for the transition. Instead of pressing on to make more Dope'Wiches, I decided to go through my Gainesville bucket list and cross off as many activities as possible.

My sizzle for pressing Dope'Wiches had faded. Perhaps the slight weight gain had something to do with it. The past year was definitely fun, and I met some awesome people around town. But it was time to press pause. Discovering how mentors can provide guidance to navigate the complexities of the working world was indispensable, since I would soon be dragged into the swirling vortex of client engagements, a consistently packed travel schedule, and tons of networking. My future mentors—complete strangers—would be the ones who would open doors for me and help me find my way closer to the world of technology and hospitality.

DANCING WITH STRANGERS

"Stay away from strangers," they always said when I was growing up. Do you remember your parents telling you that when you were a child?

I don't, but that's probably because my Hispanic Jewish helicopter mom was overbearingly *curious* about what I was doing and with whom. Despite my frustration of having to constantly check in, I did learn about the importance of recognizing who I was spending my time with. My mom always reminded me about "public relations." I didn't know what that meant until I was older. I realized that this was her way of telling me to cultivate relationships to grow my network—my network of "strangers."

Throughout childhood, we are brainwashed not to talk to strangers. Yet the second we graduate high school and go off to college, we are often put in situations where we don't know a single human. Aside from the time with family during the holidays or socializing with friends, our lives are filled with interactions with complete strangers.

What if the approach we had been taught as children was wrong? Sure, there are dangers that children need to be aware of, particularly people who approach young kids on the street, playground, or other public space. But what if our parents encouraged us to put ourselves out there in controlled environments to interact with new people? What if they realized that strangers had the ability to change the direction of our lives in a positive way, maybe more so than our closest loved ones do?

Who are the strangers we want to meet, and how do they change our lives? To help explain my claims, I will reference deep wisdom that I learned from Dr. G.

About fifty years ago, a man named Dr. Mark Granovetter wrote his thesis on a powerful idea known as the Weak Tie Theory. His research classifies the relationships in your social network into two categories. The first one, known as *strong ties*, include the people with whom you share a deep emotional bond: your parents, siblings, best friends, and extended family. Strong ties can also extend to classmates, fellow Boy/Girl Scouts, and friends from after-school sports clubs and activities. These relationships were developed through time and shared experience. Feelings of togetherness and familiarity are often associated with strong ties.

Everyone else is a stranger—sort of.

In contrast to strong ties, weak ties are people in your network whom you connect with through a mutual interest or objective. They are people you meet in jobs, classes, conferences, projects, or even while volunteering. These relationships don't have the same cohesive effect as strong ties, as we do not connect on an intimate level. While these connections don't sound as impactful, they actually provide access to new ideas, perspectives, and opportunities for growth. How so?

Entering our teen and early adult years, we begin developing our identities and figuring out what is important to us. We search for experiences that resonate with our budding interests. In this case, the bond is not as close as with friends and family (at the onset, at least). Because weak ties come from different worlds, they offer access to ideas, opportunities, and people that are completely different from those of our strong ties. Weak ties become our unofficial guides to the cross-pollination journey, directing us toward discovering our intersection of interests and skills.

Don't our loved ones want us to be successful, though? Of course, they do. But sometimes they just plain don't even know what that means. Here's an example showing such a dilemma.

Sarah is a music fanatic. She's been jamming on the guitar ever since her parents—who work in the corporate world, in fields far from the arts—signed her up for classes as a kid. When she decides that she wants to dedicate her life to music, her conservative, loving parents want to encourage her (assuming that they actually support her artistic plans, which isn't always the case with strong ties who are not risk-takers). Despite their blessings and financial support through high school, the backing she might receive is no more than a few pats on the back and words of encouragement. Although emotional support is a necessary component to success, one of the most critical factors is guidance on the steps to take to become an artist. Without direction, it is very easy to lose momentum, give up, and end up in an unfulfilling job, secretly feeling remorse for never having gone for it. But how can we go for it if we don't know how to and don't have anyone in our circle to turn to?

Whom could Sarah turn to when she needs advice on setting up concerts around town, trying to meet musicians to form a band, or searching for a teacher to learn new skills? How does she figure out answers to questions that the people closest to her know nothing about?

Enter the strangers—also known as the weak ties. These are the people we meet in classes we register for, in organizations we volunteer at, at different companies we work for, at conferences we attend, and the ones we serendipitously discover while out and about interacting in the world. They are invaluable, for they become the compass guiding us as we navigate the worlds we want to explore. With access to diverse knowledge and resources, they can point us in completely new directions. If you are lucky, you will find the person who knows just what you need to do next. If you are not that lucky but persist, you will learn through trial and error how to get to wherever you aim to go. Or you might discover a completely different path that you didn't even realize existed. All of these outcomes are better than sitting at home hoping your parents, or anyone else, will figure it out for you.

Most of the strong ties in my life were either fiercely opposed to restaurant careers (probably due to concern about the high rate of failure) or had no idea what advice to give me. I didn't have any personal connections to systems engineers or people working in hospitality technology. I didn't know they even existed. It was the people I barely knew initially who offered an introduction to someone, inspired me to join a committee, or pushed me to attend a conference. They were responsible for getting me on the path to an internship, creating a nightclub database system, or starting a food company. It was the weak who helped me find strength. It's those this book is dedicated to. It's those I hope will guide the NewBees when they show up and ask for directions.

As I prepared to enter the working world, I thought about how to continue meeting weak ties who could guide me on my cross-pollination journey. I reflected on one of the key lessons learned during my innovation class just a few months prior. Biomimicry is the borrowing of behaviors found in nature, applied to solve a problem. In this case, I would apply the behaviors of bees toward my cultivation of weak-tie relationships.

Bees make honey because it's what they eat during the winter. In preparation for hibernation, forager bees buzz about the field searching for flowers, and when they find some, return to the hive. Upon their return, the bees inform their colony where the rich sources of nectar are located. They do this by flapping their wings and starting a dance party. Really though, it's a dance known as *the waggle dance*. After space is made, the informant starts moving in an angular motion signaling the direction while shaking its abdomen to signal the distance to the source. The bees begin leaving the hive in search of the liquid gold.

As NewBees, we are constantly searching for nectar—insights, lessons learned, and takeaways—to blend into our honey—the unique viewpoint we have that makes us one of a kind. Throughout the fields that make up the stages of our lives, there are countless flowers we can extract nectar and learn from. These insights, both positive and negative, give us clarity on what we wish to include and exclude in our own journeys.

As we buzz about the flowers experiencing life, we meet countless weak ties with whom we have a chance to do our own waggle dance. We can flap our wings and ask for direction on how to continue our journey. They tell us about the next book, conference, or job where we can extract the nectar to create our honey. The information from these acquaintances gives us data that we can filter, assess, and act on. This is data our closest loved ones could have never provided us with.

The first half of *NewBee* was about cross-pollinating within environments—ones that for the most part have been guided by the decisions of our parents and the environments we were born into. The rest of the story is about what happens after entering the real world. Once we leave college, the only rules that we are bound by are the ones we subscribe to. It is our responsibility to synthesize the lessons from each experience as we continue to figure it out. It is up to us to learn the dance moves required to waggle and ask for direction when dancing with strangers.

CHAPTER FIVE
Corporate Realities

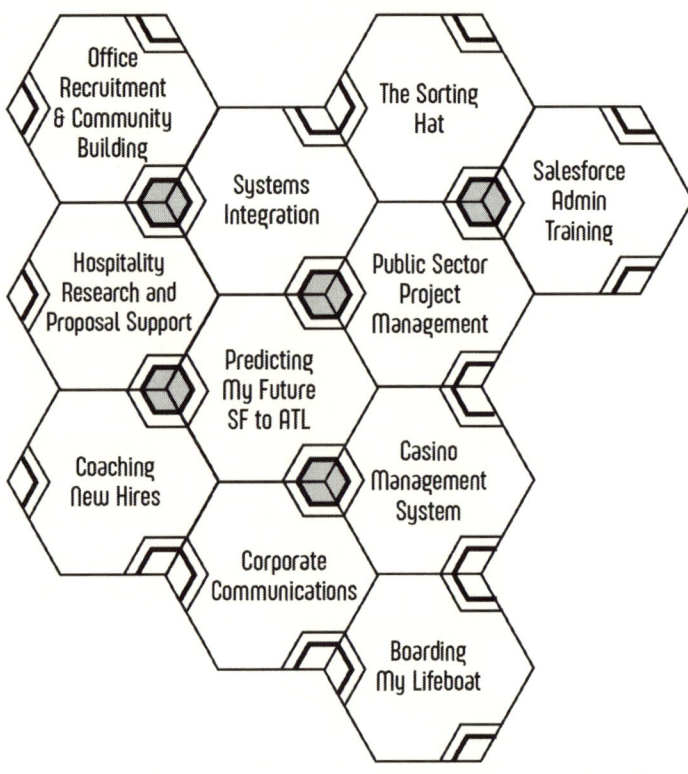

Office Recruitment & Community Building

Systems Integration

The Sorting Hat

Salesforce Admin Training

Hospitality Research and Proposal Support

Public Sector Project Management

Predicting My Future SF to ATL

Coaching New Hires

Casino Management System

Corporate Communications

Boarding My Lifeboat

When I wasn't figuring how to make the Dope'Wich become a reality the summer before to graduating, I did have a day job—an internship with B4, a privately held global technology consulting company headquartered in New York, New York. During that time, I found out that B4 had set up the technology infrastructure for one of the largest hotels in Las Vegas. Ever since that discovery, I visualized myself working on those kinds of projects, more flowers from which I could extract nectar. At the end of my internship, I received an offer and didn't think twice. I was enthusiastic to cross-pollinate at this company.

Joining a corporation provides foundational training to learn a skill set, exposes you to a ton of weak ties that can help you further your career, and teaches you how to work with diverse populations across age, ethnicity, and career stages. The foundational training I received during this phase of my life shaped who I am and how I approach my work. Along with the positive lessons learned, there were a couple of tough realities I had to face while navigating the corporate world.

The Sorting Hat

In all major corporations, there is a sorting process that assigns all incoming new hires to divisions and subdivisions according to how their skills and backgrounds match up with the varying demands across the company. Think about the scene in Harry Potter when all of the new students arrived in the banquet hall and took turns putting on the mysterious Sorting Hat that called the name of the house each student was assigned to. These assignments had huge implications for every aspect of their tenure.

A few months after graduating, I attended B4's analyst school, the training program for new hires in Dallas, Texas. Aside from meeting our fellow colleagues, this was when we discovered the results of this sorting process—a major topic of interest for new hires. Our version of the house was the functional area of the company we were grouped under, which usually determined the first project we were assigned to. When I opened up my laptop and logged in to my account for the first time, I remember seeing my house next to my name. Given my background in systems engineering, I was assigned *Systems Integration (SI)*.

I was genuinely excited by the expectation that I would be working with companies to create technology solutions that connected the dots across multiple functions of a business. However, as I started to learn more about the nature of the projects in the SI world, my feelings began to change. New hires shared stories of people who got stuck in Systems Integration for years and were unable to diversify their experience in consulting. I started to fear that my cross-pollinated nature would get obstructed and that I would end up with the same fate. There was a workshop at analyst school that discussed the process of project assignment and transfer. It would be during this session that the analysts would learn how to deal with this urban legend that spreads among every new-hire class.

One of the clichéd reasons people begin their careers in consulting is that they can get a range of exposure in multiple projects until they figure out what industry or type of work they enjoy. The reality is not always that beautiful, though—especially for folks in the SI group. Project assignments can range from a few months to multiple years. With 70 percent of incoming analysts hired into that group, it was only a matter of time before someone raised their hand.

"How does one avoid getting stuck on a long-term project?" came from someone in the back of the room.

Since B4 has been around for decades, they have perfected their project approaches. They have long-term relationships with their clients, who hire consulting firms to help modernize their technology infrastructure and operating processes. With tried-and-true approaches to getting the work done and long-term relationships between management and clients, the only missing ingredient is having reliable people who can execute the steps. While entry-level analysts and managers complete projects, new contracts are sold by the partners, which create more workstreams to transition existing teams onto. Since these existing teams already have a relationship with the client and an understanding of their processes, they are too valuable to let go. They get stuck, preventing them from ever cross-pollinating across industries.

Every analyst's nightmare.

Although we were encouraged to keep our laptops closed during the workshops so that we focused, everyone stealthily continued to check their inboxes for their project assignment. During a five-minute break, I popped mine open and stared at the bold subject line of the unread message in my inbox.

"Congratulations, your first project assignment has been assigned to you!"

I began feeling angry, disappointed, and confused.

I was staffed on the same project as my internship. I thought that B4 would have considered the request I made during my exit interview. Given that my experience was nothing more than okay—it was boring as hell—I wanted to explore what else was out there. Actually, I just wanted to avoid the industry notoriously known for trapping analysts until they leave the company. *Did I fail to mention that I was interested in hospitality?*

The moment the workshop ended, I got out of my chair and sidestepped toward the front of the room to ask for advice from the speaker on what I could do in that moment to change my assignment. He told me that the only way to override a staffing assignment is if a partner used their influence. Since I was too obsessed with pressing Dope'Wiches throughout my internship, I didn't put any time into building relationships with the partners. Mom couldn't have been more right about public relations!

He also mentioned that it was easier to get pulled out of a project by someone, rather than pushing myself out on my own. He suggested I start assisting leadership teams with business development, completing research, and any other assignments that would make me invaluable to them. This advice was similar to what John said about creating value for future mentors. My next goal would be to create a group of mentors in the hospitality practice within B4.

When staffed on a project, analysts are usually working forty to fifty hours a week on their assignments. I wondered how I would be able to become valuable to partners in the hospitality division while a doing a good job and earning a positive reputation for my own project team—yet avoiding getting trapped with my client. This led me to discover my first challenge.

The Paradox of Value

When high performance from an individual creates a reputation that prevents them from being able to transition into work that satisfies their intellectual curiosity, they become stuck in a contradiction. After spending extended time learning client needs and creating technology specifications for those needs, this person introduces risk if they want to change projects. Project leaders cannot introduce that risk to projects, since it conflicts with their own goals and targets. Because of this, leaders usually reject these requests, using bonuses and other promises to make the individuals feel less bad. Unfortunately, this sometimes happens using tactics that are not as friendly. They get stuck. This paradox poses an interesting question to newly hired members of the corporate client-service world. (For the record, I made this paradox up, but it is based on the experiences of friends, colleagues, and myself.)

Do you dive headfirst into a project assignment and risk getting stuck, or do you perform at 60 percent to develop an *average* reputation and get permission to leave, since you are nothing special? It becomes difficult to sell yourself as an *average* resource in a hypercompetitive market of exciting projects. This was the dilemma I grappled with.

The day after receiving my assignment, Nancy, the project manager, gave me a call to introduce herself, provide a project overview, and discuss my goals and objectives. My friends from the internship had warned me about the "goals" conversation. They said that the responses would be considered toward my team assignment. Nancy pushed me to join a "functional" team.

Joining a functional team offered me the chance to learn "how to develop core technology products," whatever that meant. I was warned that this was just sales talk to convince me to join a team prone to long-term assignments. My goals were not aligned with that. Fortunately, I had someone else with whom I could speak about navigating this conversation—my counselor.

Corporations sometimes pair new hires with a senior colleague to advise them when making career decisions. In this case, I needed guidance on how to not get stuck. When I shared what Nancy told me about the functional team, Joanna, my counselor, told me about another option that was available. On every project, there is a functional team and a project management office (PMO), responsible for ensuring the project is completed on time, under budget, and according to all of the specifics laid out in the contract. I had never heard of project management before.

She told me that since project management is fundamental to any project, the skills learned would be transferrable throughout my career and that PMO members could be replaced more easily than resources on functional teams. I would be able to become valuable *and* replaceable. This was the strategy I would use to navigate the Paradox of Value. It's no wonder the companies that adopt mentorship programs tend to have higher employee retention than those that don't.

When I told Nancy that I wanted to be on the project management team, she was surprised and told me that I was going to get bored quickly.

Regardless, I remained committed to my mission—I knew what I was going after.

Over the first few weeks, I started learning how work plans, schedules, budgets, resource allocation, and status reporting were used to keep our 150-plus-person project rowing in the same direction, staying aligned, on time, and on budget. Nancy was right; I got bored quickly because of the repetitive nature of the work. Despite that, I saw how my colleagues on the functional teams were spending hours upon hours figuring out the ins and outs of the core technology we were creating. It was definitely interesting, just nothing I wanted to get involved with.

I would like to highlight that whatever your first assignment might be when starting at a new company, it's important to know what you are going after. If you have no agenda of your own, you can fall victim to the countless agendas set by the different players in your company. In this case, the agenda of the project partners drives them to ensure revenues are still being generated by their resources. When preparing to introduce risks to other people's agendas, we must find a solution that makes sense for all parties. There are multiple ways to solve these conflicts. Have conversations with different people who can offer advice and perspective on how to navigate these situations and achieve your goals in the process. In my case, I had to figure out how to help the project partner generate revenue while ensuring I would have the flexibility to transfer projects— without introducing any additional risk.

Nights and Weekends

Being a part of the hospitality industry requires the sacrifice of nights and weekends. We work when people dine out, attend plays and shows, and get together with their friends and family. Although I wasn't working directly in the industry, I did have to give up many of my nights and weekends to network and explore what my company had to offer.

The moment I was assigned to my project, I began searching the internal company website (think Facebook) for any connections to the hospitality division. After a few hours of navigating through the massive site, I located the page for the hospitality team, which described some of the projects the firm had completed and the contact information for the leadership of the restaurant and foodservice subdivision. I sent an email to David, the head of the group, asking how I could get involved. To my surprise, I received a response the next day. We set up an appointment to chat a few weeks later.

By the time David and I got on the phone to discuss the hospitality team's needs, I had figured out my week-to-week routine and was fairly bored with the repetitive nature of my tasks. I told David about my experiences building the VIP system for the nightclub and pressing Dope'Wiches and shared my excitement for the industry. He told me I could help the group of practitioners leading the charge to get the group more organized internally.

B4 was serving many different clients in the hospitality space across restaurants, foodservice companies, hotels, casinos, airlines, and other subsectors in the travel industry. However, not all of the teams were in communication with one another. Joining this project management team would give me exposure to the partners working in our industry. Choosing the *boring* project management role had been the much better choice after all!

My nights and weekends were consumed by my relationship-building efforts. I was reaching out to partners and senior managers, introducing myself, researching the latest technologies that the restaurant of the future was going to require, or putting together PowerPoint presentations highlighting the projects that B4 had completed globally. I focused on creating value for people, in the hopes of creating a mentorship relationship, which would eventually convert into project work.

As the weeks went by, analysts and consultants joined our team, and we produced materials that the senior leadership team used to create new business proposals or research papers. David had been thanking me for my contributions yet cautioned me that the project work being sold was for the strategy division of the firm. Being a part of the technology division, it wasn't likely that I could cross the invisible line separating our divisions and join those teams. I continued to help nonetheless, having faith that I could convince someone to give me a shot. Heeding his warning, though, I started planting seeds in other gardens to increase my chances of finding project work—cross-pollinating across other areas of the company.

Reflecting on my experience building the CRM system for the nightclub, I realized that I was working for a company that built similar solutions for clients in other industries. There was an entire subdivision dedicated to developing CRM systems. By partnering with market leaders in the CRM space, such as Salesforce, Oracle, and SAP, B4 had developed processes to teach their employees exactly how to build these systems using a proprietary step-by-step approach. Being in a different subdivision than CRM, the only way for me to learn more about how these systems were built and maintained was to enroll in a training course. I chose to learn Salesforce, since it had free training available versus the other platforms' courses that cost thousands of dollars. Completing the course taught me the fundamentals of how a Salesforce system worked, which would be extremely beneficial for me in the future. After finishing this initial training, other initiatives with community development and mentorship—two of my personal priorities—started to pick up in the New York office.

When the opportunity arose to join a local office committee, it was a no-brainer to join the culinary committee that brought in food vendors for various events throughout the year. My first event was a breakfast for the college seniors who had been given an offer and needed a little extra convincing when they visited the office. Instead of bland corporate catering, I convinced the office recruiter to let me splurge on a Belgian waffle breakfast bar to seduce our guests. Food definitely has that power. After organizing that event and developing a relationship with the New York City recruiter, she put me in touch with the national recruitment team that organized the new-hire training program. She recommended me to apply as a coach at the next analyst school. A few weeks later, I was awarded a spot to serve as a mentor for the upcoming new-hire class.

I was truly surprised at all of the doors that were opening by employing the tools I loved: using food to create community and mentorship opportunities.

Despite the doors these "side hustles" were opening up for me, none of them were full-time project opportunities. In companies across the corporate landscape, employee performance is assessed based on standardized goals and targets, which results in compensation adjustments and feedback sessions to determine how you are doing. At B4, we were encouraged to set goals in areas that included community service, local office development, training, recruiting, and last but certainly not least, business development. Although encouraged to think about these other areas of our careers, the main objective we were assessed on was our billable-hours ratio—how many hours spent on client work out of total hours worked. (Hint to newly hired professional services employees: billable hours are usually *far* fewer than the number of hours worked.) This is one of the many ways companies with high turnover design their performance-evaluation process for new hires coming out of college. If the average tenure of analysts is two to three years, companies must design a system such that both the company and the employee can maximize value while minimizing risk. A couple of the many reasons for this two- to three-year tenure are the pursuit of an MBA degree and/or getting stuck on a long-term project and eventually finding a job in an industry that employees (think) they are more attracted to.

In the eyes of the company, none of my side hustles mattered, since my real goal was billable hours. They were a means to an end—project work within the hospitality or CRM industry. I needed to find a spot on a project that would let me charge billable hours. A lifeboat would eventually appear.

Boarding My Lifeboat

About eight months into the job, I started becoming bitter. I had been receiving great reviews from my boss, had met almost every single partner in the hospitality group, became engrained in the New York City office community, and completed training courses in the CRM division. I felt like I was doing everything I should to get pulled out of my current assignment. Feeling sad about the constant setbacks, I relied on my support group of friends to motivate me to keep pushing forward.

My situation wasn't unique. Most millennials deal with the same situation—being assigned to an area that does not align with their professional interests. My friends and I continued supporting each other by sending leads for new projects, training resources, and memes—lots and lots of memes. We were trying to get a huge corporation to change for our little desires—no easy feat. We had to keep a smile on and have fun.

Although I was disappointed at every letdown, I needed to believe that something would emerge. I wouldn't realize it, but everything I learned while stuck in project management work would be invaluable years later. In our careers, especially at a young age, we sometimes feel like we are in a blind alley, spending weeks, month or even years working on projects that we don't like. As Steve Jobs famously said, "You have to trust that the dots will somehow connect in your future." The lessons learned while in these alleys return to your benefit years later. Everything happens for a reason.

Toward the end of the summer, I was sent an assignment that needed to be done in under twenty-four hours. Not a huge deal since it was PowerPoint slide formatting for a proposal—a skill you get quite good at when you dedicate your nights and weekends to it. I shared the update with Nancy, in hopes of receiving her support if we won.

"Of course, Ernesto! I'm super happy for you, and I support your pursuit. Just remember, though, that most proposals are lost." My emotional state prevented me from discerning if I actually had her support or not.

Turns out that we defied the odds and won the engagement. The team let me know that there was a spot for me if my project approved my release. Even though Nancy was willing to go to bat for me, she still needed to get approval from the project partner. Whatever she said must have worked. Thoughts became things. Visualizing my future on a hospitality project manifested into reality.

All aboard! Weeks later, I was boarding a cruise ship for my next project. Our team was hired to figure out how a modernized casino-management system could improve communication between various teams and enhance the player experience. Sounded like they wanted to create the Ritz-Carlton Mystique.

During this new project, I was splitting my time between my new life in New York and my past life in Miami, staying with my parents. One of the weekends I was home, I met up with my sister, whom I hadn't seen in over a year. She had lost sixty pounds, looked fantastic, and had an exuberant energy. *What happened?* She told me about her visit with a "seer" (cue image of those shady five-dollar palm-reading signs you see around town) who shared what her path had in store for her. Sounded pretty ... *out there*. Two hundred dollars later, I was sitting in the hot seat, curious to see how my future in hospitality technology was going to unfold.

Adee, the seer, had told me a few things while we were together. Two of them really stood out. The first is that she didn't believe food was going to be my end goal. She saw me working in education technology. That could be true, but it was also a pretty general statement. The second thing she told me was that I needed to go to San Francisco to figure out why Atlanta was the next step in my journey. Those were some pretty specific instructions. I had nothing to lose by introducing a little spontaneity into my life. Besides, I had a couple of friends in San Francisco who spoke highly of the city. I was on the lookout for the weekend to make the pilgrimage.

The casino technology project was super fascinating. The downside was that this project was barely ten weeks long. By week five, we started preparing the final presentation. With my upcoming availability showing up in the scheduling tool, the staffing managers in my division started reaching out, asking if I had another project lined up.

Right around this time, I was notified that B4 won a multimillion-dollar systems integration project with a restaurant client. In the email, I saw the proposed project team that had a spot for an analyst. After reaching out to the project team, asking if I could join them, they told me that the analyst would be brought on at a later phase. Ugh, that would have been a dream come true. I told the staffing managers that I was still searching for my next project.

Since I was assigned to help the project partner on my casino project create the final presentation, I had a few more weeks to continue developing our relationship and figure out my next gig. After I shared my angst with him, he asked his colleagues if they had any open roles.

"Government projects were always in need of analysts ☺," my staffing manager would remind me (yes, with smiley-face emojis—I did not like her). I started to panic at the thought of getting back on a train to my old project and getting stuck. Having a spot as a coach at analyst school did give me an extra two weeks to find a project. *Thank you, unknowable forces of the universe, for giving me extra time to figure this out.*

The national recruitment teams that offered me a spot as an onboarding coach reached out to schedule my travel for the upcoming analyst school. On the return home from the program, I booked a multicity trip to SanFran, hoping that magic would happen before I returned to New York. Going to analyst school gave me a chance to share my perspective and adventures with the new hires, demonstrating that it was possible to move around the firm and vary their time there. Despite my enthusiasm while sharing my story, I was still without a project and secretly experiencing an existential crisis.

As the weekend program ended and I boarded the bus to the airport, I received a call from the partner I had just finished working for.

"Call Simon and tell him about your passion for the industry. Good luck."

Simon was another partner helping a hotel company improve how they developed technology internally. I told him about my experience with the nightclub, the cruise project, and my larger involvement with the firm's hospitality practice. When he asked what I was doing on Monday, I told him that I was flying back from San Francisco.

"How quickly can you be in Atlanta?" he asked. I froze. Then, I remembered to wish him a good weekend and hang up the phone.

Holy guacamole! (Extremely PG reaction to how I felt in that moment.)

One weekend and three flights later, I landed in Atlanta and took an Uber to the headquarters of one of the largest hotel companies in the world. Upon arriving, I met the rest of the team and awaited instructions. We had been hired to understand the process of taking ideas to live products and recommend ways to improve it. As an example, if they wanted to add a new component to the reservation page on the website, we had to outline the process that they would take to ensure that was done successfully. It wasn't the most exciting work, but I was relieved to remain within the hospitality teams for a few months at least.

The following week, I received a message from one of the new hires I met at analyst school.

"I'm on the coolest project! You would love this!" Receiving that message was the sign I was waiting for, what Adee had predicted would happen in Atlanta. It was time to abandon ship, board my lifeboat, and leave the firm.

When I was told that the new restaurant project was not going to bring on an analyst, I thought their reasoning was sound, since analysts usually join projects at more mature phases. However, when I was asking a friend of mine for any leads for new projects, she told me that she was asked if she wanted to join that same team. Although slightly annoyed at the favoritism, I reminded myself that she had an extra year of experience and had worked closely with that manager who was leading the project— two significant advantages. Because she was leaving the firm to work for another company though, she told me that she would put in a good word. Alas, no luck. I had to look elsewhere, leading me on my enigmatic journey to Atlanta.

Guess which project that new hire was staffed on. She was brought on because she lived in the same city the client was based in, so her expenses would not have to be charged to the client. Also, as a new hire, her time was not billable, which generated huge savings for that client. After learning these stipulations with her staffing, I understood why the decision was made. However, I would have appreciated transparent communication from the beginning. The staffing manager for that restaurant project was coincidentally also the restaurant technology leader for the firm. I was not inspired to learn about the intersection of restaurants and technology with this person, especially if he didn't feel like he could communicate with me.

This was one of my early lessons regarding transparency in the business world. Although pundits say clear communication is a key to success, it rarely happens properly. Corporations, especially large ones, will always have complicated communication styles, especially since people in general struggle with the skill. I'll never know why he didn't tell me the realities of the project. What I did know was that I didn't want to work with someone who didn't feel he could communicate with me.

Through cross-pollinating my efforts in multiple areas, I have found success in discovering new ways to meet new people and organizations. My stories at B4 show how the Law of Attraction mysteriously operated in the background, manifesting opportunities to continue my exploratory journey. The timing for this miscommunication aligned with an opportunity to leave B4 and join a multi-concept restaurant group in need of an analyst to set up its technology infrastructure to keep track of sales, inventory, and labor, the critical components of a restaurant business. Although I didn't have direct hands-on experience with that, my future boss had faith that I would figure it out. Someone I was excited to learn from.

They say overnight successes are a myth. People (and the media) only notice when someone has become news- or gossip-worthy in one way or another. They weren't paying attention to the long months and years of preparation, learning, and trying. Like success, change works in similar ways, often over extremely long periods of time. While the new job opportunity, interview, and transition occurred in a few weeks, the process began years before, when I decided to launch a bakery inside my college apartment. By attempting to use my systems engineering tools to continue improving my process, I was able to start a business that created and sustained a new passion for modernizing tradition. Never would I have anticipated all that followed from developing a curiosity for learning how to make french toast from scratch!

CHAPTER SIX
Baking Up New Beginnings

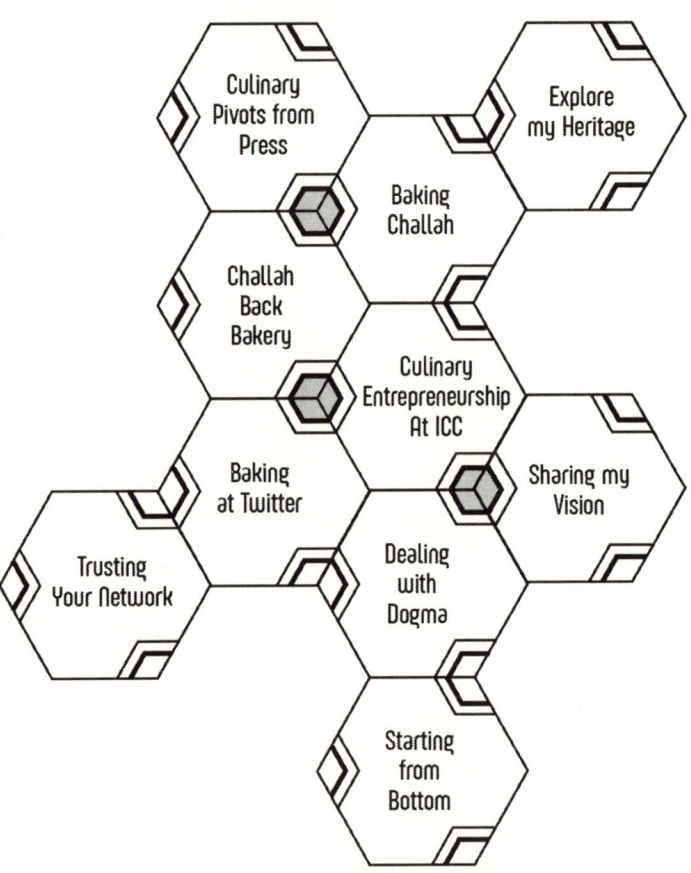

Years ago, when I invented the Dope'wich, I felt like I had created the dessert world's greatest treasure. Every time a person sunk their teeth into the fluffy icy-hot creamy delicacy, their facial expression embodied my hypothesis. After a few catering events, I started to think about what else I could incorporate into the Press model. I iterated the sandwiches using brownies, cinnamon rolls, and even cookies in place of the donuts. All of them were way too decadent. Then inspiration hit again.

What if I pressed a french toast breakfast sandwich? What if I used challah bread to make it? I was Jewish, and challah was a part of the traditional weekly routine of Shabbat dinner. This could be a chance for me to cross-pollinate my heritage with my love for food and creating an experience for others to enjoy.

My rabbi advised me to connect with his wife, who made challah on a weekly basis. Going through my challah apprenticeship taught me the fundamentals of making the Jewish staple. Learning traditional baking techniques gave me great joy. However, I am always looking to modernize traditions. Trying to cross-pollinate my approaches in this situation made me realize that not everyone shares the same attitude with respect to change.

"So, I was wondering if we could change things up?" I asked her. We used the same toppings week in, week out, and I was getting tired of the sesame seed/poppy seed combo.

"What did you have in mind?"

"Let's throw some Oreo cookies in there!"

"Oh, we can't do that. It's not allowed!"

I was confused. Was I breaking the rules somehow? Oreos are definitely kosher.

"It's just that Oreos are not Cholov Yisroel." This was new vocab for me. This was an extra level of laws that applies to dairy products. (Ironically, Oreos are dairy-free. But she didn't know that, and I didn't know that.)

Alas, that's what apprenticeships are for: Extract the nectar. Transfer the pollen. Create new products.

I went home and made my first batch of Oreo challah, and gifted them to two of my mentors. I was encouraged to put my bread on the market. @challabackbakery was launched then and there on the 'gram. The next Friday, six customers placed orders for Oreo Challah. It was the end of my college experience, and I had only a few more weeks to experiment. I would press pause, knowing that I would continue baking challah to create feelings of joy once I was settled in New York City.

Bringing Challah Back

Weeks into the start of my consulting experience at B4, I started to get the hang of my somewhat regular "routine." I traveled Monday through Thursday for work and spent the little time I had left building my personal life, which included regular stints of at-home baking in preparation for the Shabbat dinners where challah would be served. All my friends told me that I needed to get Challah Back Bakery up and running again.

While B4 offered me the chance to learn more about the hospitality industry, the research assignments I completed for the hospitality teams weren't exactly the hands-on experience I was craving. Even when I shifted over to the projects in the hospitality space, the scope was limited to the creation and management of technology solutions for those businesses. Challah Back Bakery would give me the opportunity to get my hands dirty with the end-to-end business: sales and marketing, production and delivery, finance and accounting, and, of course, technology.

Since Fridays are known to be optional work-from-home days in the consulting industry, I restarted my efforts at building my at-home bakery business. I searched Google on how to grow a bakery business out of my apartment.

My search results flooded my internet browser with sponsored ads over the next few days. One of these was for the International Culinary Center's (ICC) Culinary Entrepreneurship program. With an alumni roster that included several culinary superstars such as Bobby Flay, David Chang, and Michael Chernow, I knew this was the real deal. The Culinary Entrepreneurship program was a sixteen-week course that taught the foundational components of a food business. This course would help me create the foundation for my challah bakery. The only barrier to entry, though, was the $10,000 ticket price.

Invest in Your Education

One of the perks of going to an in-state university is that I didn't have to pay the high prices that out-of-state or private universities charged. My parents told me that when it came to grad school, they would help me out since I paid for my college education with scholarships. What if I could convince them that this program would be my version of grad school?

One lengthy argument later, I was back at square one. They thought I was quitting the opportunity that B4 was giving me. It didn't matter. Although the course was very expensive, I was convinced it was the next flower in my journey. The school did not offer payment plans for programs outside of the core culinary degree, so I had a few weeks to find the funds before registration closed. Two days before the deadline, I used a freshly minted line of credit to pay for the course. One $10,000 loan later, I was ready to get my ass in the seat.

"Getting asses in the seats is our number-one job as restaurateurs," the first speaker kicked off the course.

Chuckles came from the audience.

"Our second job is to restore those who walk through our doors with food, beverage, and hospitality. The root of the word *restaurant* comes from the French *restaurer*, meaning *to restore*. Every week, dynamic leaders from the New York hospitality industry came in to share their wisdom and teach us about the different aspects of the business: recipe costing, employee management, kitchen design, business law, branding, service models, finance and accounting, etc. They regaled us with their personal stories that applied to the lessons of the week. The lesson plan for each class was structured with the assumption that students would apply the material to their own concepts. Every week, we were responsible for submitting a completed business plan that would be reviewed by the instructors to keep us accountable.

Each class gave us the chance to ask questions about different applications of the lessons. Whether we were a catering service, a bakery, or a quick-service restaurant, the answers to the questions usually overlapped across all concept types. Between my bakery-specific questions and the loaves of my challah I brought to class, I would become known as the "Challah Man." I couldn't pass up the chance to share my product with the leaders of the industry. Pro tip: Sharing food is almost a guaranteed way to get people to like you.

The class was ten weeks long, sessions running from 9 a.m. to 4 p.m., with a one-hour break where we ate a family meal. During lunch, I would approach the instructors and ask a few personal follow-up questions. I wanted their advice on how I could get into the industry. More specifically, how could I apply my background in systems engineering into the restaurant world? I didn't expect these interactions to cause the friction that resulted.

Starting from a Different Bottom

The first time I posed my question, I was told that I needed to become a server in order to learn the operation. This response brought me back to my days as a busboy while in college. While taking classes in computer programming and automation, I would think about how restaurants could apply the concepts I learned. When I had a few moments after my shifts as a busboy, I would ask the general manager how they used their customer databases to create tailored marketing campaigns or how they analyzed their sales mix to influence the rotation of menu items. He'd tell me to get back to clearing tables. Years later, I thought that my instructors would have a better answer. Unfortunately, that was not the case.

I was advised to pick up shifts as a host on the weekends at a restaurant. I was not interested in learning about dealing with customers, managing employees, understanding food and wine pairings, or the operations of a restaurant. Rather, I wanted to learn how databases optimize and automate the back-end infrastructure of a restaurant. Man, I thought that one of the sixteen instructors would have a lead for me. I kept getting the same response. I needed to "start at the bottom."

As a general rule, the suggestion was certainly not wrong, but I wanted to climb up a different ladder. I was starting at a different bottom and was looking for a ladder that didn't really exist—in their worlds, at least. While these leaders probably felt like I was trying to shortcut the system, I only wanted to capitalize on my strengths and nerd out on the data produced from the operation. Either I wasn't clearly articulating how I wanted to break into the business, or the restaurateurs didn't know how systems engineering applied to restaurants. After all, we came from completely different worlds. I didn't want to burn bridges with anyone, so I would always politely thank them for their insight and shift the topic of conversation back to the lesson they taught the class.

At the end of the course, the class coordinator filled champagne flutes for us to make a toast. With a glass in one hand and a certificate of completion in the other, we now had (official) permission to take over the culinary world!

Trusting Your Network

At the conclusion of my course, I was still assigned to the government project at B4, frantically searching for ways to transition into the hospitality world. With projects continuing to fall through, I needed to figure out how to alchemize my disappointments into new energies. Restarting Challah Back Bakery was the perfect project to achieve this transformation of emotions. I posted on my social networks that I would start delivering freshly baked loaves of challah to customers around New York City.

The first week, one of my customers, Wally, asked me to deliver his order to his office. Moments later, I found myself riding up the elevator to the fourth floor of the headquarters for Twitter. Since it was late, the office was empty except for Wally and his boss. When I showed his boss the goods, she asked if I could bring her a challah the next time I stopped by. The following week, I had six orders come from the office. Week after week, I returned with more and more bags filled with challah bread. Since I only had one destination to deliver to, I was able to increase my production to over twenty loaves. I became known as the "Challah Dude" on Wally's floor. Even the receptionists and security guards started to order from me.

On one of my visits, I had an extra loaf in my bag. Wally suggested I leave it on the corner desk at the edge of the room. *Why not.* A few days later, I received an email from someone named Mike, who thanked me. He was interested in hearing my story and wanted to meet for breakfast. Thinking it was another young professional who was eager to get into the food business, I happily agreed and set up a time and place. Weeks later, I found myself at a bar celebrating a friend's birthday, when Wally sent me a text message: "You ready for tomorrow, man?" I was surprised and wasn't sure what was special about the meet and greet. I started getting nervous when he followed up with, "Do you know who you are meeting?" After pulling up LinkedIn, I realized I was meeting a senior vice president. I had never met someone that senior who was interested in *me. What would we talk about?* I immediately started chugging water and made my way home to prepare for the morning meeting.

Walking into the Thompson Hotel in SoHo, my heart started beating relentlessly. Matt was waiting for me in the bar area with a breadbasket for us. His warm personality extinguished my anxieties. *So where do we begin?* After I shared how my pursuit of the intersection between restaurants and technology led me to bread baking, Matt started asking questions. He sincerely believed that my product could be one of the next food sensations in the city. He wanted to help champion the Challah Back cause. I was grateful for his praise and began sharing my alternate plans.

Feeling rejected by the people I was working with most closely at B4, I had started looking for a job where I could apply what I had learned from my consulting and baking experiences to restaurant operations. There was a prominent farm-to-table fast-casual company that was hiring for their rotational leadership program. Mike urged me to consider that I would learn exponentially more if I committed 100 percent of my time to figuring out how to create a system to grow my product and my following.

The truth of the matter is that I was petrified of failure. Having been told my whole life that I needed to have stability with a salaried job to support myself and my future family had a tremendous influence on my decision-making and risk tolerance. Mike shared his story of how his experiences with failures led to his current success.

"When your network sees that you are a hard-working individual who is making things happen, they do whatever is in their power to help you succeed," he told me. The day after losing his job at his prior company, his network sent him three interview opportunities. I think he was trying to teach me about the mysterious ways in which the universe operates. The story resonated with me, as I have had my fair share of serendipity, where I am left utterly dumbfounded by the opportunities the universe creates. Aside from sharing his personal stories, Mike offered to introduce me to his friends who led companies throughout the city and to prominent investors at venture capital funds. This was an offer that seemed too good to refuse. Meeting Mike and listening to his proposal put me at another major fork in the road.

While I was baking challah for team Twitter, I had been working with one of my instructors from the Culinary Entrepreneurship course on a mini-project to help the company that she started working for. That project led to a new job that would enable me to jump into the world of restaurants, technology, and analytics. Between the choice of the entrepreneurial unknown with the support of Matt, and a salaried job that allowed me to continue cross-pollinating, I chose to put my carb-loaded dreams on pause to start at the bottom of the ladder I had been searching for my entire life.

CHAPTER SEVEN
Pollinating in the Startup World

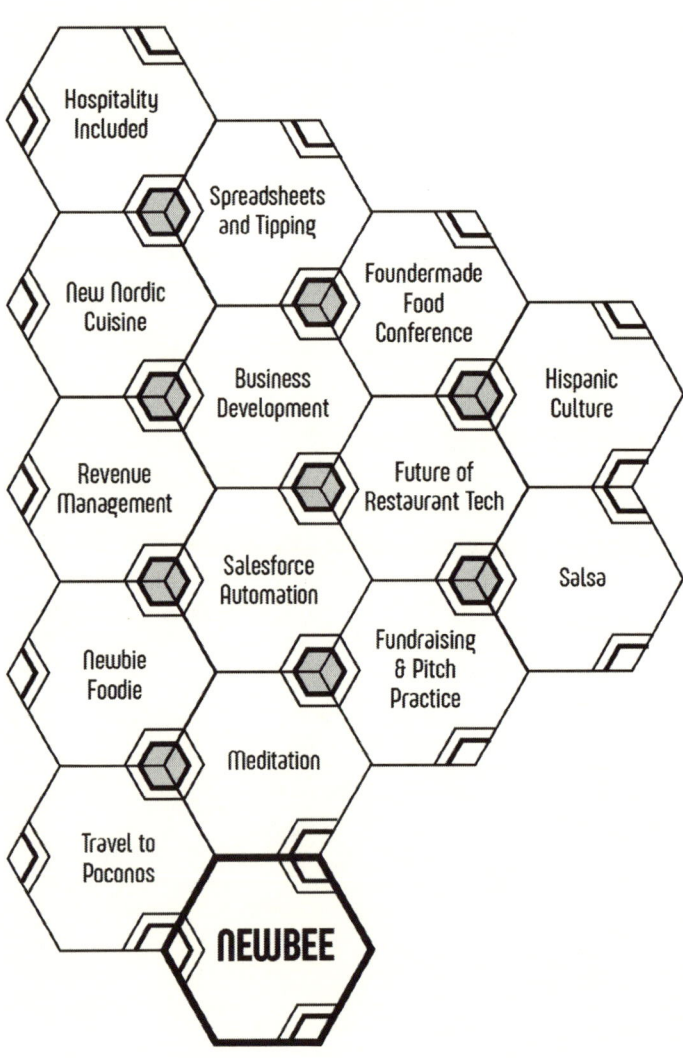

Cross-pollinating in the hospitality space had become my obsession. At B4, if I wasn't completing my day-to-day project assignments, I was supporting senior leaders with initiatives within the hotel and restaurant subsectors. Outside of work, I had been baking challah in my apartment and networking with restaurant professionals. I read books about the food business and couldn't seem to watch anything other than food shows like *Chef's Table* or *Ugly Delicious* on Netflix. I was relentlessly searching for my next flower in the field of restaurant technology.

Six months after the entrepreneurship course concluded, I sent a round of Happy Holiday emails to my instructors. One of them, Tracy, wrote back to me asking if I could help them build a tip calculator. A prominent New York–based restaurateur had eliminated tips in his restaurants, launching the "Hospitality Included" service model to create more comparable pay between the kitchen and the dining room. Tracy needed to figure out how her new restaurant group could create their own tool that would distribute tips to their staff. Since this was new for the restaurant world, it was an opportune time to put my spreadsheet skills to use. I enthusiastically agreed to help them figure it out.

A few days after sending my work in, I received an email introduction to her boss, John, the chief operating officer of Dansk, a newly formed Danish restaurant group. John asked about my background and why I wanted to get into restaurants. After I shared the journey I had been on, attempting to combine systems engineering and restaurants, John dove right into his pitch on how I could analyze the data within the systems the company had set up in order to manage the businesses they were launching. It was a match made in heaven—or the universe—or whatever transcendental place you believe in.

As the operations analyst, I was going to be responsible for analyzing the data generated by the systems supporting the business. To provide reliable analysis, I had to ensure that the systems had been set up properly, which would take up the majority of my time. Additionally, I was tasked with supporting the executive team by creating forecasts for new business opportunities and project management. Although my B4 PMO experience seemed incredibly boring, repetitive, and downright useless at the time, it would serve me tremendously in this new role juggling multiple projects.

As a NewBee without much experience in analysis work, I was constantly second-guessing myself and relying on my superiors to help guide me toward the solutions. Because I was able to stay organized with my assignments, they would want to help me or point me to resources where I could learn more. Most of the time, I had to figure things out on my own. There weren't as many websites that taught the analytics work I was doing as there were coding schools that taught people how to build apps and websites. Venturing out of your comfort zone and trying to get experience without experience can be daunting for anybody.

When it came to my intersection of restaurants, technology, and analysis, I started realizing there was a gap in educational resources—blogs, courses, conferences—available for the self-starting newbies who wanted to learn more. The subject matter was limited to those with years of experience, and it was kept in their heads. No one had productized that knowledge. I had to rely on the vendors to teach us their individual solutions, which usually didn't take into account the rest of the technology tools their system had to play nice with. Recognizing this led me to kick off a personal project called "Newbie Foodie," which showcased people who brought their experiences into the food industry, creating unique products and services. In my case, it was going to be an educational product that taught restaurant professionals about restaurant technology and analytics.

While I was working at B4, I had attended a restaurant technology conference to look for companies that were making an impact in the space. Revoire, a point of sale (iPads used at coffee shops and retail stores) company, led a workshop about the future of restaurant technology. At that moment, I remember checking if they had any jobs available. Almost a year later, Revoire came back on the scene, as they wanted their platform to power a nonprofit project that Dansk was launching in Brooklyn. Throughout the sales process, I became interested in the company's growth plan and asked to meet with the CEO to learn more. After hearing their story and explaining to Neil (the CEO) what I had been working on, he started to sell me on why I needed to join him in his conquest to revolutionize the industry. He promised that I would get to study every data point in the restaurant and teach others the insights learned from the information, eventually becoming a thought leader in restaurant analysis. I was mesmerized by the idea of helping create an educational platform to narrow the gap in resources for restaurant analysts and spread technology literacy across the industry.

Both of these companies gave me opportunities to deepen my understanding of how I could continue to cross-pollinate my passions. Although startups have quite the appeal—stock options, meditation rooms, treadmill desks, happy hours, and several other perks—there is always a tradeoff with every choice made. These two startups were still very early in their development, which generated chaos, uncertainty, and anxiety in my life. When first introduced to both environments, I always gravitated to my safety net—standardizing databases and systems.

Start-Up Systems

Dansk was a Danish food-and-beverage empire that launched a food hall, a fine-dining restaurant, a bakery, a kitchen production facility, a coffee roastery, and a number of cafes around the city at the same time. With over fifteen hundred ingredients being used across five hundred menu items, the company needed to use an enterprise resource planner (ERP) to monitor operations across the company. ERPs are used to track operational and financial data within a business. Since I was coming from the world of technology implementation, John took a gamble that my background and experience would enable me to bridge the gap between the day-to-day operational processes and the financial analysis of the business. As he said, I would be the systems engineer of the company, discovering opportunities to improve the operation. On day one, I opened my laptop and fired up the program. It was blank. When I asked John where the information was, he smiled and said, "Welcome to Dansk." I was hired to set this up and put the company on a path to success. Classic bait and switch.

As a newbie, I had to rely on my previous experience. In school, I had learned how these systems conceptually helped businesses make decisions. Then I tried to build out my own tool for the nightclub. But now it was time for the real test. By no means was this one person's responsibility, which is why companies like B4 are hired to tackle these large implementations. Following the same approach we used with our clients, I began reaching out to the different teams across the company to learn about their day-to-day process and get familiar with the information they needed to complete their tasks and fulfill their job responsibilities, "gathering business requirements," as they called it in the consulting world. The end goal was to program the inventory and recipe items into the system so that management could understand their actual vs. theoretical food cost and usage.

Having a system to keep track of purchases, usage, and waste is one of the critical measures that restaurants implement to monitor their inventory, roughly 30 percent of the costs in their business. It would normally take about two months to set up a system for our business. However, since our CEO and founder was a New Nordic culinarian who strived to create innovative food and beverage products, the constantly changing recipes prevented me from stabilizing our inventory system. Similar to how the retail industry changes clothes according to the weather, restaurant concepts rotate menus according to what produce is being harvested throughout the year. Every two to three months, the effort that I put toward setting up the recipes in our system would go to waste because we had to replace our recipes. Instead of changing one component within a base recipe, say from blueberries to raspberries in our muffins, a completely new muffin recipe was created. I understood that we needed to incorporate some element of change. I just didn't understand why we didn't modify something small like the garnish or the sides that were served with entrees. These small changes required constant reprogramming in our inventory systems, which further delayed the completion.

After a few seasons, I began losing patience. Although I was learning a tremendous amount about inventory-management systems from this project, the CEO was not slowing down his change requests. I'm a devout believer in adapting to your environment. But I couldn't stand how little attention was being given to the work required to monitor these changes, to measure whether or not they were even successful. When Revoire appeared on the scene, I felt that since the company was closing its Series A round of funding (a major milestone for tech startups), things would be different. I would soon learn that *not all that glitters is gold*.

Before joining the company, I was told they had wrapped up the funding round. However, once I joined, I learned that the investors still had questions on a few KPIs (key performance indicators) needed to make their decision. I helped the team quickly pull together figures such as monthly revenues, number of leads in our sales pipeline, number of restaurants that would be on the platform in the next six months, the company headcount, and runway—the amount of time before running out of money. In a perfect world, all of this information resides in a company's ERP, their accounting and operations system. Startups rarely have the funds or resources to set up and maintain expensive ERPs. They rely on extracting data from the multiple systems they use.

Revoire used Salesforce, one of the leading CRM platforms in the market, to keep track of current and future clients. Because of the Salesforce courses I had taken while at B4, I was familiar with how the system should be set up. Our system was not in a good place, because the data had no integrity—it was not up to date. After we were able to get back to those investors and raise money to continue growing the company, I told Neil that I would dedicate my time to fixing the system so we could automate our reporting and have answers readily available when we needed them in the future.

I was no expert at Salesforce, but I did realize that we weren't using any of the automation capabilities the system offered. I did my best to create rules that enabled the system to store key pieces of data throughout the sales and setup processes for each account.

After several weeks, we finally had a tool that was able to help us generate the reports used to communicate with potential investors, customers, internal teams, and the media. With everyone speaking the same language, communication was vastly improved.

The startup systems were essential to answer the questions that management teams at both companies were asking. One of the benefits of setting up systems like the ERP at Dansk or the CRM at Revoire was exposure to multiple areas of both businesses. Having an understanding of what every department was working on was essential to programming the system to represent reality and, ultimately, connect the dots.

Exposure to Multiple Areas of a Business

Since startups tend to take on too many projects with too little time and money to deliver on them, the people working in them have to stretch their skill set across teams. Because of my project-management experience at B4, I took the unofficial role of project manager at both companies, ensuring that the different teams were staying on track to complete their tasks. In addition to supporting the project-management function and setting up systems, I used spreadsheet modeling to create forecasting models and created training materials for employees.

John asked me to learn new businesses every few weeks. First, there was the butcher shop. Then, a dairy production facility with cheeses and *skyr*—Icelandic yogurt. There was even wholesale bakery and coffee bean distribution. It was like a crash course into a food MBA program. Since our founder was kind of famous in the food world, he was constantly bombarded with partnership opportunities. It was up to me to put together financial models outlining estimated revenues and costs associated with all of these programs. Putting together these projections was another first for me. I had to enroll the chief financial officer and ask him for guidance in creating forecast models that would answer the questions the team needed clarity on in order to make a decision. Although my recommendations were sometimes disregarded, I was glad that I had the chance to go through a culinary MBA program. Even though our projects required many late nights, we had some perks. I was always given boxes of freshly baked, "defective" loaves of *rugbrod* (rye bread), spandauers (OG Danish pastries), and sourdough boules to take home whenever I visited the bakery. *Every company has its perks!* Before shifting to Revoire, I was told there would be a similar MBA-style training program to expose me to the different parts of the business.

Boot camp was the six-week onboarding program to learn about the problem we were solving, the customers we were serving, our industry, and ultimately how our point-of-sale solution was going to change the game. In theory, it was a comprehensive introduction to the company. In reality, the program did not exist. When I asked my colleagues where the information was, I never got a straight answer. Or they would point to the whiteboards with outlines of our processes, with three-word descriptions for each step. Without any documentation, I volunteered to organize the information into a PowerPoint presentation, like the documents I spent nights and weekends putting together at B4. Working on this project required that I meet with every department in the company to understand how they did what they needed to do. Speaking to members of each department made me recognize how people with diverse working styles and personalities can come together to achieve a group mission. Unfortunately, I was never able to finish the document, since I was asked to focus on fundraising, which required me to clean up the system to report on the KPIs. The way that money plays a role in driving priorities was a new insight that I picked up while working in the startup world.

While at both companies, I asked John and Neil if I could help them out with investor relations. Both were happy to teach me how to create investor presentations, how to keep track of the investments made, and how to create effective communications to update our investors. At one point, I was even given the chance to pitch directly to investment analysts who wanted to learn more about the companies. (I didn't close any deals, but it was great practice.) Since I had hopes of starting my own company one day, pitching a business was a critical skill to learn. I would need to raise money and/or develop partnerships when I was further along in my journey. Like the coursework completed while working B4, it is extremely beneficial to take advantage of your environments and expose yourself to these educational moments.

Being in the room with owners and company directors enabled me to take part in interesting conversations that dictated the course of our organizations. While I enjoyed being in the know, I also started to realize some of the not-so-sexy patterns within startups—specifically how the need for money, pleasing customers, or courting important investors can drive the agenda for growing organizations. The level of change and iteration we went through on a daily basis taught me about what it really meant for startups to roll with the punches.

Rolling with the [Startup] Punches

For startups and new businesses, the need to adapt is a reality that every-one has to get comfortable with. (People are not excused from this reality either.) Usually, the founders or CEOs lead the charge, due to an insight inspired by a conversation with a customer, an investor, or a colleague. While the need for change is usually warranted, the context or reasoning isn't always clearly communicated, which can cause frustration. In both companies, our visionary founders would constantly change the priorities for what menu items to create, which software features to build, or which new business opportunity they wanted to chase. The excuse of keeping up was typically that "we had to roll with the punches." I was complaining inside because I saw what was happening, and I was left to rework all the programming in our systems to ensure accurate reporting would be maintained.

At Dansk, the management team was competing against the New York City culinary elite for our CEO's attention. Since everyone and their mother wanted to collab with Dansk, we were flooded with requests to sell beverages, chocolates, spices, and other retail items into the different parts of the empire he was building. While I was working tirelessly to analyze and understand how each of these opportunities translated into dollars and cents for the business, I would eventually discover that decisions were made without my recommendation. Although it felt like I was wasting my time, I would encourage myself with the reminder that this was a good learning experience.

At the peak of my frustration, I had a mental breakthrough that would lead me to refocus my energies on the idea of educating others on how technology could be used to keep up with the constant change in the industry. I started to write my book, *Newbie Foodie*, which was not only going to share the importance of outsiders coming into the industry but also document everything I had learned to date on restaurant technology and systems engineering. I aimed to pass my knowledge along to the next group of analysis professionals entering the restaurant world. This revelation intersected with my stumbling into Revoire, a company that shared the common vision for technology education. Coincidence? I think not.

When I originally started working at Revoire, I was given the book *The Hard Thing about Hard Things* by Ben Horowitz to introduce me to what it was like to be a CEO of a technology startup. The main takeaway was that there is no rule book for how to successfully run a startup. It's a constant barrage of issues and problems that a CEO has to reallocate the available resources to fix. Not having visibility into the full picture and being asked to keep up can cause frustration for team members. However, being the right hand of the CEO exposed me to some of this crazed reality. Outside of work, I was trying to help Neil keep his head above water, even walking his dogs home on days when he was tied up in meetings. Although at times I felt like an intern fetching coffee, I knew that helping Neil with the little details of his day would be a tremendous help for him. Maybe I didn't need to open myself up to that, but hindsight is 20/20.

One of the hard things described in the book was keeping up with customer demands. This became very concrete after seeing it in real life. When almost all customers are considered "A-listers," it's difficult to determine what the priority should be. If we promised someone that a specific feature would be developed, we needed to do whatever we could to make this happen. Sometimes, these customers were investors, which gave them extra weight over the other customers we served. No matter what the data from the system showed, these were some of the political factors behind the punches we had to roll with. As the CEO's right hand, it became a bit difficult for me to remain excited about my work, because no matter how efficient the system I created to help us become more streamlined, there was always a reason to make exceptions.

Work environments directly impact our feelings of happiness, satisfaction, stress, anxiety, and boredom. Ultimately, they impact our self-esteem, leading to an increase or decrease in our productivity levels. Leading companies around the world design their environments to maximize the productivity and fulfillment of their employees, to keep them motivated by their work and connected to the larger vision. Young startups rarely have the resources or the bandwidth to solve for this intangible problem, which sometimes results in burnout for their employees. I wasn't necessarily being overworked like an investment banker, but my motivation was definitely diminishing.

It became challenging for me to stay excited about my work at both companies, since I didn't feel my contributions were valued or had any impact. The deliverables I produced were either disregarded or overruled by other priorities. Similar to how I used my baking to stay sane while at B4, I turned to my hobbies to unplug from the day-to-day, in hopes of generating inspiring ideas and fresh perspective.

Cross-Pollinating Hobbies and Desires

My hobbies introduced me to new ideas. Cooking food evolved into creating community. Learning computer coding became building VIP-tracking software. Pressing Dope'Wiches and baking challah turned into hosting dinner parties and meeting executives. Even though I enjoyed cross-pollinating while on the job, I started to recognize how cross-pollinating my personal interests while off the clock led to some pretty cool personal discoveries. To continue this practice, I needed to create boundaries to make time for these hobbies in my life.

Meditation and running were two activities that protected my sanity throughout the stressful times at work. Meditation began as a seated practice and eventually transitioned into an active one—running—for extended amounts of time, which created the "flow state." Motivated by the physical challenge of completing a marathon, I registered for the Miami Marathon, which forced me to make time to train. In both running and meditation sessions, the goal is to become aware of the flurry of thoughts our crazy minds bring to the forefront and reroute our attention to the activity we were engaged in—running or breathing deeply. Both of these practices enabled me to connect with myself and understand what my mind was preoccupied with. When I started marathon training, I enlisted my girlfriend to run with me. Running together gave us time to talk and come up with some interesting ideas.

We ran around the city on weekends. Over many months, we had dreamt up some pretty ambitious plans. We joked about opening a hostel in Colombia one day, inspired by the vibes that the Broken Shaker concept in Miami created. The dream was out there, until it manifested into something very real. On one of our runs, we ran into an old friend who told us about another friend who was in South America working for a company building hostels for digital nomads. The universe had manifested yet another opportunity for us. I reached out and set up a time to learn more.

The company was hiring people who increased and decreased the daily rates of the hostels to maximize profitability (think of surge pricing on Ubers while busy or airfare and hotels during holiday weekends). Even though I wasn't particularly interested in revenue management, I took an introductory course that led to a breakthrough. The course basically taught me how to use Excel to do the job efficiently. I remember thinking *What if this existed for the restaurant industry?* What if there was a course out there that could teach servers and chefs how spreadsheet tools can be used to understand their businesses better? The chefs at Dansk always joked that they were terrible with numbers—maybe this course could be the tool that helped them improve their skills. This kicked off my desire to create my first educational product for those interested in restaurant analysis. Had it not been for my running habits and my short-lived dream about the hostel world, I probably would have never had this breakthrough. I eventually stopped pursuing the hostel company. Soon after, Revoire reappeared in my life.

It had been years since graduating from college, a period in my life that was filled with Hispanic flair from the Society of Hispanic Professional Engineers. Growing up, I always wanted to learn how to dance salsa and merengue. Because of the unpredictable nature of my traveling schedule during my consulting days, it was impossible to commit to class during the week. Now that I wasn't traveling, I had more of a grip on my schedule. When Kevin, one of my best friends from college, told me about a salsa offer he purchased on Groupon, it was a no-brainer. I cleared my schedule on Saturdays for class.

Salsa class was an awesome break from the day-to-day grind. It was also challenging, as we had to learn how to move our feet to the beat, lead our partners through different twists and turns, and maintain a pace that followed the rhythm. After months of attending class, I started to see the parallels between leadership on the dance floor in the studio with leadership in life.

One of the key tenets of dancing is using distinct physical cues to lead partners through the movements. It is the leader's responsibility to understand their partner's skill level and adjust accordingly. If leaders are not clear with their direction, then the follower is not exactly sure where the dance is headed. Talented followers sometimes get frustrated and "back lead," creating their own moves by forcing turns and removing the action-reaction dynamic found in dancing. Etiquette states that at the end of the dance, dancers break away and search for new partners.

At work, our bosses are the leaders we choose to get on the dance floor with. These leaders have the responsibility to understand where their followers are at regarding both skills and emotional mindset. The day-to-day grind of dancing together requires efficient feedback loops through communicating with each other to create a remarkable dance in which both parties feel fulfilled.

"So, let's meet up tomorrow morning to finish up this presentation?" Neil asked me on Friday afternoons in preparation for the following week's investor meeting.

"Uh …" Did I really have a choice here? The projects I worked on with him were always critical to raise cash, the lifeblood of the startup.

"Sure, but I have salsa at one." I ensured he was aware of my boundaries.

"I know, *salsa boy*," he would joke with me, shimmying his shoulders with a smirk.

Neil always wanted to work on weekends. It was hard for me to tell him that I did not want to work on Saturdays, so I used class as an excuse— even though it would have been totally fair to tell him how I really felt. There was one weekend though when I didn't work or go to salsa class. Kevin and I gathered a group of friends to get out of the city and hang in the Pocono Mountains.

We rented a cabin, hiked in the woods, built fires, and shared stories from our lives. When it became my turn to talk, I opened up about *Newbie Foodie*, the book I had started working on.

I shared how I wanted to use my story to inspire others to weave different experiences in their lives and apply them to the food industry. The mezcal started to really kick in, and I began rambling about the idea that life is a set of interconnected experiences that are linked and filtered through our long-term desires and ambitions. I shared how I used the Law of Attraction to manifest experiences that resonated with the future I wanted to create.

As I was explaining this to my friends, I started reflecting on the original message I wanted to convey with the book. While *Newbie Foodie* was about encouraging outsiders to get into the food industry, the overarching principle is about discovering how your passions and curiosities can be woven into your career to create a fulfilling experience. My specific story was about combining the power of food and hospitality to create community in my life and educational products to teach others about analysis. It was a lesson taught to me from the behaviors of bees.

On the road to the mountains, I was reading a series of articles on biomimicry, a discipline within the study of innovation that borrows patterns found in the natural world. One of the animals profiled was the bee. Bees have to make honey to survive the winter. This process starts with bees extracting nectar from flowers. While doing so, they also transfer pollen from flower to flower, enabling flowers to create fruit that have the seeds needed to eventually reproduce. (Fun fact: bees are responsible for the creation of over 30 percent of fruits and vegetables that we eat.) After the bees return to the hive, they deposit the nectar, and honey is eventually created. There are lessons that we, as humans, must learn from the bees.

We have to extract nectar from the many different flowers in our lives. The jobs and companies we work for, the courses we take, the conferences we attend—all of these flowers provide us with nectar we take back to the hive to create a unique honey or point of view. All the while, we transfer these insights across the organizations we involve ourselves in, enabling those organizations to benefit from innovative solutions created elsewhere.

Since each of us has a unique set of interests and passions, the journey we go through is one of a kind. We are all NewBees, developing distinct perspectives in our own subject area. At the time, I felt like the idea was mind-blowing, or maybe it was just the mezcal. Feeling inspired, with a new message I wanted to share, I felt that I had to repurpose my project to speak to a larger audience.

Ever since returning from that trip, something wasn't right. I couldn't stop thinking about how I wanted to share the message of cross-pollination as my truth.

Over the next few months, my job with Revoire stalled out. I couldn't find cross-pollination opportunities within the organization. Reflecting on the leadership lessons from salsa class, I realized that Neil and I were not dancing to the same beat, and I couldn't focus any longer.

Leading in salsa is simple. The leader is responsible for just one person in front of them. Leading organizations becomes exponentially more difficult, as they have the responsibility of setting the mission, vision, and values to align a tribe of customers, employees, and investors. Just like every subtle wrist movement in dance, every one of these decisions must inspire their tribe to follow them toward a future they are creating with the organization.

When I felt that I didn't want to dance anymore at Revoire, I decided I would wait until the end of the song and find the next partner to dance with-the next steps in my journey. With a desire to finish crystallizing my message on cross-pollination and organize it into this book, I resigned. I decided that it would be best to leave New York City, move back with my parents in Florida, and figure out how to self-publish *NewBee*. I could never have predicted the universe's alternate plans for me.

CHAPTER EIGHT
The Pollination Paradox

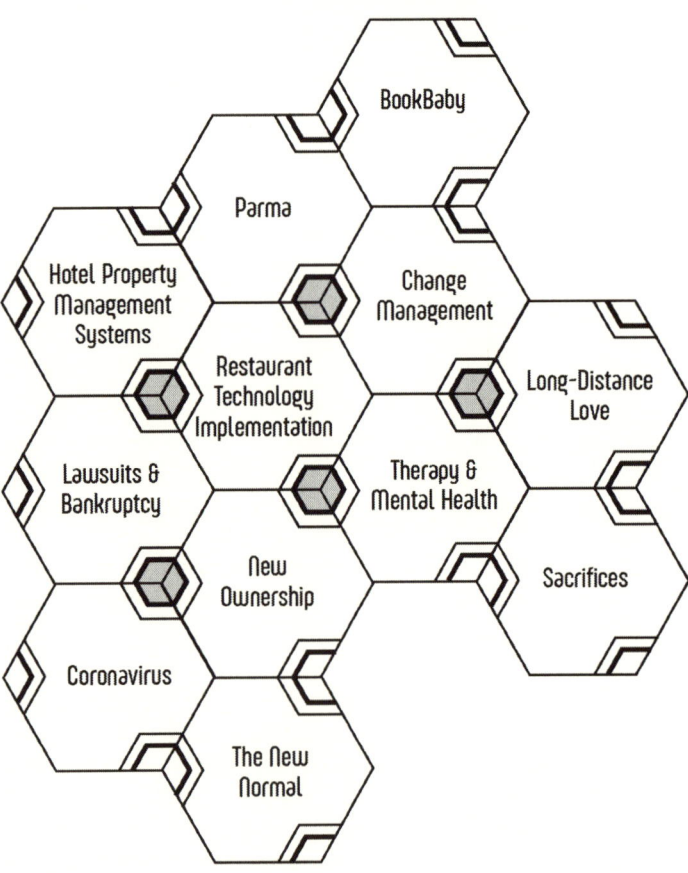

BookBaby

Parma

Hotel Property
Management
Systems

Change
Management

Restaurant
Technology
Implementation

Long-Distance
Love

Lawsuits &
Bankruptcy

Therapy &
Mental Health

New
Ownership

Sacrifices

Coronavirus

The New
Normal

Years ago, when I went to work in Erie, Pennsylvania, I declared that I was never going to let a corporation dictate the direction of my life—such a naïve and overly proud millennial I was back then. Since making that declaration, I steered my life toward New York City, built a community of friends, found hobbies outside of work, and created a cross-pollinated career that spanned restaurants, technology, and systems engineering.

Before leaving New York, I was presented with an opportunity that challenged the declaration I had made years ago. This job was described to me as another "peak" opportunity where I would be able to transfer all the pollen I had picked up over the years, causing an organizational rebirth, and potentially write a follow-up book about it. Taking the job made sense—it was the manifestation of creating another career experience that blended my passions, interests, and skills. Even though the eighteen months that followed were filled with personal and professional breakthroughs, I would also experience my deepest depression, leading me to recognize the true role that cross-pollination plays in our lives.

Last-Minute Changes

Au Revoir, *Revoire*. I was fired up about my renewed direction. The plan was to move back to Miami, finish the book, and travel the country to speak about cross-pollination. Even though I intended to manifest these incredible ideas, the universe had a few last-minute changes in store for me.

With a few weeks left in New York City, I spent my mornings writing and my evenings checking off my bucket list: seeing the sights, eating the eats, and drinking the drinks at all the places I never had time to enjoy. To add some extra spice into my last few weeks, I mixed my adventures with online dating. When Lauren, the first girl I matched with, told me she worked in the beverage world, I knew I found a suitable candidate for a bar crawl down Avenue C, one of the bar-lined streets in the youthful East Village.

Five bars and several cocktails later, we were at Pouring Ribbons, ending the night and chugging several glasses of water to prevent hangovers the next day. After a deeply passionate good-night kiss, my heart was swirling with a mix of emotions that included but were certainly not limited to: excitement, confusion, and frustration. *What the f&*$. Of course, I would meet an epic chick weeks before transplanting my life.*

The next night, I was having dinner with John, my boss from Dansk. John had been on a global culinary expedition, eating a different cuisine every two to three days for the past few months. We continued the tour at a Malaysian restaurant in Chinatown.

"So, what are you going to do?"

"I'm moving to Florida in a few weeks, finishing my book, and buying a van to drive across the country and speak about cross-pollination to university students! I'm going to teach them how to discover their intersection and create their own careers." I was energized.

He was happy that I was still working on the book but seemed to have missed the road trip plan totally.

"Well, that's great ... but what if I have a job for you?"

He noticed my unhappy expression.

"You don't even know what I have to offer. I want you to write your next book about this experience."

Just under a year ago, another charismatic visionary had said the exact same thing to me. John was responsible for giving me a shot in the food industry, so I owed him to at least a hearing.

"Have you ever heard of Parma?"

For those unfamiliar, Parma was a family-owned steakhouse that started over ninety years ago. It is a quintessential steakhouse joint that has grown over the years. John was being tapped to refresh the organization with new technology solutions that would make it more efficient.

"I want you to come with me and lead the change," he said.

Who, me? What the hell did I know about company turnarounds?

"The company has grown to over twenty units and has had quite the run. Despite their growth, they've been struggling with cashflow and have finally decided to look outside their circle for some help. I want to bring you with me because I think your combination of skills and experiences is the fresh perspective the company needs to reinvent itself. It is your chance to leave your mark on such an iconic institution."

Hmm ... combination of skills and experiences ...

"Let me get back to you."

The job would require me to move to Washington, DC, and then eventually Orlando, as part of a corporate relocation. Was I about to pick up and move my life—twice—to take this job? My declarations were so naïve. Sometimes, jobs require us to make sacrifices—especially dream jobs.

After speaking with several mentors, advisors, and friends, I concluded that my plans to travel around the country could be put on pause. There was no way I could pass up the opportunity to reinvent one of the oldest family-run institutions in the restaurant world. I called John and told him I was in.

Despite my decision to leave New York, Lauren and I continued dating and spending time together. All our moments were fun and exciting, amplified by her witty humor and my high energy. We didn't love having to start a long-distance relationship but hated the thought of breaking up just because we lived in different cities. We wouldn't be the first or last couple to be in a long-distance relationship. There were plenty of buses and trains between New York and DC—it wasn't such a bad setup. After a few months of dating, it was time for me to head to our nation's capital.

Outsiders Looking In

I was incredibly stoked to be joining Parma, an iconic steakhouse that was one of the gathering places for businesspeople, celebrities, and politicians. This was my moment to apply all the lessons I had learned from the flowers I had been extracting nectar from throughout my career. It was the peak opportunity for me to revamp an organization with the perspectives I had gained regarding communication and collaboration, implementing technology systems, and teaching others how to analyze their business. Coming into the company as an outsider reminded me of my favorite scene from *The Alchemist*.

The Alchemist tells the story of Santiago, a Spanish shepherd, who journeys to the Great Pyramids of Egypt in search of a treasure. Along the way, he finds himself at an oasis, speaking to the leaders of a tribe who had been wandering the desert their whole lives. When Santiago shared the warnings from a vision, the leaders laughed at him, questioning why they—the ones who lived their whole lives in the desert—had never had such visions. He explained to them that as an outsider, his eyes had not become accustomed to the desert. He was able to see from a different perspective. As an outsider, I noticed several opportunities for how to immediately improve the business. Convincing the desert leaders of my new tribe, who had decades of experience, to listen to my ideas would be a challenge I definitely would struggle with.

There were several issues that were immediately apparent when the new team arrived at headquarters. The main one (and usual suspect) was communication. There were plenty of emails being sent and telephone conversations being had between people; however, there wasn't a shared understanding of progress on projects, action items, and open issues. This would threaten the companywide transformation that was on the horizon. Despite best practices on introducing change, especially in old-school environments, we were forced to get going right from the get-go. The crazy eighteen-month-long roller coaster ride was just getting started.

In my second month on the job, an article from a famed food publication announced a nine-figure payout that was awarded due to a family feud at the iconic steakhouse. The dispute was between the owners, but the media made it seem like the restaurants were in serious trouble. I thought my job was over—and I was not alone. The entire organization, from the corporate office to the restaurants and the guest base, started to panic. Most of the employees in the company, who had had lifetime tenures, had never dealt with a situation like this. John, who was used to dealing with emotion-filled organizations and complicated situations, immediately set in motion what we needed to do over the next day, week, and month.

New momentum started to form—yet I was fearful. After sharing my concerns with John, he asked me to trust him and to help keep the team coordinated on executing his instructions. I had to surrender and have faith that the universe had my back. While the thought of quitting certainly came to mind, I have always strongly felt that every experience in life is a test. The company was not bankrupt, and I was still receiving my paycheck. Ahead of me was a huge restaurant technology-transformation project, arguably what I had been working toward my entire career. I couldn't let a spur-of-the-moment emotion derail my decision-making logic.

The next few days were filled with drafting press releases, holding conference calls with general managers, and sending emails to our guests. Through coordinated action and communication with the external world, we would demonstrate that Parma was still in a position of strength. With the need to quickly organize different projects, I immediately implemented project-management tools I had used in prior jobs, which would enable management to monitor what each department was working on. The first tool introduced was an instant-messaging platform that let team members message each other or participate in group discussion on certain topics. The second was a digital sticky note board that contained cards symbolizing action items different teams needed to complete. Since many of our team members were traveling to the different restaurants around the country, these two tools allowed everyone to stay informed on project updates, who was accountable for what, and when they were due.

Now that we had set up our internal tools, we began to introduce new initiatives to the outside world. These included year-round seasonal menus, an incentivized holiday gift card program, a refreshed beverage program, and new digital programs. While our food was "timeless," introducing the year-round seasonality enabled our chefs to experiment with new recipes and offer our guests new items, which increased the frequency that they visited the restaurant. The holiday gift card program offered a new incentivized bonus structure that awarded an extra $25 for every $250 spent. This led to a record-breaking sales promotion. After minting partnerships with new high-end beverage brands, we refreshed our cocktail list with inspired twists on our classics. We also partnered with credit card rewards programs and corporations to motivate new customers to check us out. Launching all of these initiatives required our team to perform at the highest levels, not missing a single email or deadline.

As the project manager responsible for keeping the master schedule, I relied on my meditation habits to keep my cool, day in and day out. I complemented my morning meditations with intensive gym workouts, which prepared me for the frenzy of tasks, activities, and meetings that came with each day. On the weekends, I would either travel to New York to visit Lauren and hang out with friends, or she would come visit me in DC. Despite having six-hour bus rides on the bookends of my weekends, those retreats were rejuvenating.

The new team was cross-pollinating at Parma, bringing everything that they had learned throughout their careers into our timeless institution. One of my colleagues told me we had changed more in ten months than the previous ten years. Despite the number of external positive indicators that included positive same-store sales, increased loyalty memberships, decreased turnover, and increased guest frequency, a negative mood was beginning to develop among the corporate team members. After completing the initial sales and marketing projects, the transformation shifted to the overhaul of the technology systems and eventual outsourcing of support functions of the business. This transformation was going to disrupt the lives of employees who had been working at Parma for decades.

Parma's Paradox

Change management is arguably one of the most difficult (and profitable) services to offer for companies that need to transform. Our team was facing the cognitive biases and habit patterns engrained in the team over decades. Living through this exposed me to learn how organizations could be blinded by their own success.

Parma was never a technology-forward company. They never really needed to be. They were wildly successful, and the owners were making profits for decades. Why try to fix something that wasn't broken? Although not my personal belief, that is probably what went through their minds over the years. The owners never made investments in technology-literacy training or incorporated it into the company culture. While I was grateful for this—since it led to the need for modernizing technology and my eventual job—it made the adoption of new tools and systems difficult. I could not understand why it was so hard for some of our team members to log in to a meeting or print a report. *Was I doing something wrong?*

The company was split into two factions. There was the old guard, which included family members and loyal colleagues who had been with the company for decades. Then there was us—the newbies—who had been hired to change everything. The groups clashed a lot. The old guard used passive-aggressive resistance to thwart any new initiative we proposed. Every time I met with any of them to discuss a new project, I felt that they must be thinking, *Who the hell is this kid in the orange glasses telling me what I'm doing is wrong?*

After completing a few initial projects, I realized that none of the old guard was using any of the project management tools I created. My ego was pissed. Why spend all this time to have my efforts ignored? Eventually, I learned that they were just not used to working like this. For decades, they could work on whatever they needed to without anyone challenging them. Here I was trying to revolutionize how they had worked their entire lives and getting flustered because they didn't immediately conform. I was being an unreasonable gratification-seeking millennial.

In addition to changing their working styles, we also realized that there was a different set of orders being sent from the top. Needing funds to pay for the lawsuit, the owners did whatever they could to generate more sales, which meant organizing private wine dinners or pop-up specials. Split between listening to management and listening to signers of their paychecks, it became obvious that they chose the latter.

The environment I was working in was extremely convoluted. It was a shit show. Going into this job, I expected it to be the "ultimate" experience.

I thought I was hired to bring my set of experiences to cross-pollinate my ideas at Parma and give it fresh life. What I could never predict was the amount of resistance I would be forced to strategically maneuver through. People didn't enjoy the change and projected their insecurities onto me (and everyone else). I wasn't able to deflect their stress and started questioning the value of my contribution. I felt so much self-doubt that I began to crave external validation. It was during these moments of internal despair that I looked back at my days at B4 with appreciation.

Companies like B4 implement processes to keep their massive legions of employees motivated and engaged through the use of feedback and validation. Employees constantly receive feedback on a weekly, monthly, quarterly, and annual basis. Bosses and managers are constantly letting direct reports know if they are doing a great job and rewarding them for it or explaining why and how they need to course correct. Smaller businesses—especially ones that are "old school"—don't have the time or the structured process to conduct this back-and-forth. So, I had to try and seek it out myself.

John continued to reinforce that I had been doing an incredible job. With the end-to-end technology implementation about to begin, he told me to try to focus on that project—it would be my capstone career project. He knew the environment we were in was chaotic and would chat with me about the struggles we were both facing. He was my therapist at work.

As I continued growing my understanding of how the dots connected within restaurant systems, there was a *disconnect* that started to form within me. The paradoxes within my work environment had generated tremendous anxiety that was bleeding into my personal life. I eventually realized that I was stuck within my own paradox.

The Pollination Paradox

Eight years ago, I had made a decision not to let a company dictate where I was going to live my life. What I didn't realize back then was that companies don't make these decisions. We do. Based on the demands of their business, companies present job offers with responsibilities, salary packages, benefits, and a number of other considerations. When I was initially presented with the offer to join Parma, I was focusing on the shiny objects—the fancy title and salary. Let's not forget "how good this would look" on my résumé. I had fallen in love with the story of how this fit into the grand scheme of my pollinated journey. What I didn't realize existed were those "other considerations" that came along with this job—what I was giving up in exchange for taking this role.

My mental health began slowly crumbling a few months into the job. I wasn't able to maintain my personal boundaries. I could barely take a break when I left the office, since I received calls from restaurant managers with any number of questions on where to find reports or how to fix issues. I was never able to get restful sleep due to my spreadsheet-filled dreams that caused me to wake up every night. I had to do something about my downward spiral. I had always heard that therapists help people sort out their mess. Perhaps it was time to enlist some professional assistance.

Having never been to therapy, I had no idea where to begin. Between asking my friends and searching the internet, I found a practice I'd take a chance on. Talking with a professional who was able to offer a neutral perspective on the changing dynamics of my life was incredibly helpful. I was able to begin understanding the source of my feelings and emotional triggers. After a number of sessions, I diagnosed that the cause of my shaken-up mental state was due to the "Pollination Paradox."

Throughout my entire life, my parents had stressed the importance of keeping a safe, stable job—common advice from our strong ties. This belief that had been subconsciously ingrained in me influenced my decision-making when it came to my career, ensuring that there was always guaranteed pay through a salaried job. At heart, I am a creative who has devised an innovative method that enabled me to learn about my passions within the confines of corporate safety. However, the most recent decision to cross-pollinate at Parma resulted in my being deprived of the things I held closest in my life: friends, family, and community. The Pollination Paradox was the result of elevating the external motivations ("fulfilling" career experience) above my internal hierarchy of needs.

Lauren had been a great support in dealing with my trials and tribulations. We shared memorable moments together traveling, eating at cool restaurants, hanging out with friends, and spending time with family. I had developed a dependence on those good experiences to feel better about the chaos in my head, which led to forming terrible codependent tendencies. I eventually learned it is never a partner's job to make the other fulfilled.

With the arrival of summer, additional changes and anxieties were on the horizon, including the move from Washington, DC to Orlando. Orlando had been the elephant in the room with Lauren and me since the beginning. The stress from the move was apparent now more than ever, evidenced by our mini-flare-ups and arguments over the tiniest disagreements. Eventually, we both realized that although we had a wonderful time together, there was a disconnect with our communication styles and what we wanted long term. Although it stung in the short term, separation would be the best option for both of us.

All my life, I had been pollinating for the sake of creating the "dream job." While I could argue that I was successful, I wasn't paying attention to the true aim of cross-pollination. Putting so much emphasis on this dream job resulted in neglecting what I needed to create the dream life, where a job is just one component. Coming out of another aha moment, I started to think about how I would reevaluate this breakthrough with my definition for cross-pollination. The move to Orlando would provide the time and space needed to reflect and reset.

Starting Over

When I was in B4, stuck in that government project for months, Nancy taught me a very important lesson: sometimes life requires us to start over completely. Events will transpire that force us to reconsider our decisions, reflect on our choices, and reinvent how we approach our lives. The move to Orlando was a moment when I would heed her advice and begin considering what I wanted to manifest. To create new energies in my personal life, I began waking up, working out, and starting the day at 5 a.m., preparing my meals following ayurvedic nutritional guidelines, extending my meditation practice to forty minutes per day, and trying to limit consumption of stimulants such as alcohol and caffeine. Aiming to rebuild my sense of community, I signed up for a class at a small salsa studio, joined a nearby gym, and found a synagogue for young professionals that was across the street from our office. The move was turning out to be not so dreadful after all.

We started to wrap up the technology transformation heading into the holiday season. Our gift card campaign had been running for a month, and we were beating the prior year's record-breaking sale with several weeks remaining in our promotion. The restaurants were busy, we were making money, and we started to get excited that we finally were ready to manage the business effectively in 2020.

Although my time at Parma was insanely stressful, it offered me the chance to experience what I always wanted to do: transform an organization through implementing modern technology and educating restaurant professionals on how technology can be used to analyze their business.

One of the stark contrasts between the two halves of this book is the mention of using a vision board. Since I entered the professional world, I stopped maintaining a physical vision board. It evolved into more of a directional focus at the intersection of restaurants, hospitality, and systems engineering. Perhaps it was time to change my approach. Feeling nostalgic for my younger years, I decided to take a blank piece of paper and think about the pictures I needed to create a new vision board for the cross-pollinated life I wanted to create.

For the first time in my life, I decided not to search maniacally for the next flower. Instead, I opted to appreciate the flight that I was presently floating through.

THE NEW NORMAL

Wouldn't that have been just the cutest bee ending ever? I wish it would have been that adorable as well.

Remember that lawsuit?

While John was good at keeping everyone focused on completing the organizational transformation, he didn't have any influence over the family members arguing over the payment that was awarded as part of the lawsuit.

While the management team had their hands full with the technology implementation, months passed without any resolution on the legal front. As the technology implementation was wrapping up, another headline hit the wire: "Judge Clears Sale of Parma." This had definitely ballooned into more than a back-and-forth between family members.

In the days that followed, I found out that the company would be sold in the next three months, we were projected to run out of money in the next thirty days, John was leaving the company, and I was going to be coordinating with lawyers and bankers to get this done. *What the hell did I know about selling companies?*

Here I was, faced with yet another situation without prior experience. I had no time to stress about my inexperience and continued to remind myself of all the times I had to leave my comfort zone. By this point, I realized that my ability to ask questions to figure out how to complete the task at hand was my greatest skill, and it would help me get through this.

Over the next three months, I got a taste of the investment banking life and confirmed that I was never going to do well in the field that everyone thought would be a great career path. Those teams worked at all hours of the night and on weekends—definitely not the life I wanted to live. After weeks of putting together data, presenting to potential buyers, and navigating the complex sale process, the eventual purchaser was one of the largest privately held restaurant groups in the country.

Based in Houston, Texas, the purchaser owned more than eight hundred restaurants, five hotels and casinos, and an NBA sports team. Prior to the sale, Jaime, my VP of operations, who used to work for this company, had been telling me about his former colleague who oversaw the operational analysis division of the company. This division was responsible for analyzing every number across the organization, in search of opportunities for improvement. These were the systems engineers within the restaurant world. *Restaurant systems engineers existed after all!*

He was excited for me because I would finally get to work on what I had been searching for my entire life. Now that I had figured out how to use my honey to create a dream job, it was time to figure out that dream life part.

The acquisition paperwork was signed, sealed, and approved at midnight, March 10. Over the next few days, the NBA canceled their season, Disney World and Universal Studios closed the parks, and cities around the country restricted restaurants from offering dine-in service. The world was going through an unprecedented transformation due to the effects of COVID-19. Coronavirus was forcing hundreds of millions of people to radically change their understanding of what normal life was. In the weeks that followed, the economy would freeze up, the stock market would drop 30 percent, companies would drastically slash their costs, and millions of people would be furloughed. The world was ending.

At the beginning of quarantine, restaurants did what they needed to do to survive: turning themselves into grocery stores, launching meal kits, setting up delivery programs, selling gift cards at a discount, auctioning off unique dining experiences, and whatever else to drum up cash to keep afloat. The restaurant industry, the second-largest private employer, with over fifteen million people, was decimated, with hundreds of thousands of stores closing. Even though the government would step in and create enormous aid packages to help industries and consumers, it simply was not enough to get us back to where we once were. It was an incredibly stressful time, as every news outlet covered the apocalypse of life as we had always known it.

Socioeconomic commentators, consultants, and industry analysts have all agreed that the pandemic will result in a rebirth of society—a "new normal" for businesses, nonprofit organizations, governments, and the rest of the world. Everyone will need to have the courage and willingness to completely reinvent themselves. Maybe everyone needs to have that conversation I had with Nancy about starting over, with themselves.

After the deal had closed, Jaime told me that my future boss didn't think I was going to last long. *What the hell? This was my dream job! Who was he to judge me so quickly?*

My new boss was right. After helping our new owners integrate our technology systems into theirs, I resigned. With my reinterpretation of how cross-pollination fit into my life, I decided that I was not going to move to Texas. Despite having created a dream job and being in a recessionary environment, I needed to stay true to my principles, surrender to the universe, and have faith that new opportunities that fit into the vision board of my life would manifest. I am done with prioritizing my career as the driving force for my life's direction.

Before I left, I asked him why he made that statement months ago. He told me that I seemed like someone who couldn't sit still. He knew that the analysts on the team lived and breathed spreadsheets all day, every day. Without the freedom to cross-pollinate across departments, transferring insights, and contributing to the honey our organization was creating, it was never going to work out for me.

Never could I have imagined the journey that having the desire to own six restaurants would take me on. Along with the rest of the world, I had to hit the reset button and figure out how I was going to live in the new normal. With the honey I have spent years creating, I wonder about how I can best contribute to the world as we begin creating this new normal all together.

EPILOGUE
Final Thoughts on Cross-Pollination

Cross-pollinating my life has given me the chance to work in a variety of companies, to interact with interesting humans, learn many cool things, and become a more flexible problem-solver. It has taught me to become a more adaptable person in this world. The crazy revelation that I have at the conclusion of this writing is that I discovered cross-pollination through pursuing my dream and recognizing the fear while doing so.

Answering one of the most significant questions of my life has required me to figure out how to face my fears of pursuing entrepreneurship while maintaining the structure and stability that all of my loved ones and strong ties ardently recommended ever since I was a child.

Looking back on my journey, I identify the many different forks in the road, where I had the option of surrendering to the universe and embracing the entrepreneurial path as I tried to open a restaurant, launch a digital challah bakery, move to South America, or even take a road trip around the country. Instead, I opted for the safer route, holding on to my fears, yet finding a way to dress up my jobs and create an intention around them to fit into the narrative of combining my skills and passions to create a fulfilling career.

One of my role models, who has built a career out of facing her fears, speaks about the tremendous lessons learned when choosing to acknowledge the fears and developing comfort with them. She did a hundred-day project where she faced a fear on a daily basis, learning lessons through each experience. Throughout my journey, I have discovered my own tactics to dance with the fears and make progress in my journey.

While cross-pollination and my exploratory approach to living have enabled me to answer my question on career fulfillment, it has also been the justification for my delay in embodying entrepreneurship—creating unique products and services using my honey to improve our world.

As we reach the end of this book, I share a few final thoughts on cross-pollination.

Identifying the [Intangible] Checklist

In my early days of consulting, a close friend gave me key advice when assessing the opportunities at B4. He told me I should think about the fifteen to twenty skills I would need by the time I became an [aspirational career title]. So, if I wanted to be a partner at the company—or a technologist, a restaurant owner, a teacher—I should list the skills I needed to acquire, then seek out experiences where I would learn those skills. It was great advice, except there was one issue.

I don't think I ever had a checklist in front of me that said if you do these fifteen things, you will become a successful restaurateur, a restaurant technologist, or a technology educator. As evidenced throughout my story, our visions for what we want to do will go through several iterations. When we ask other people for advice on how to pursue our goals, they will provide their own version of the checklist filtered through their own journey. The advice I received was never bad, but I had to adjust based on what my gut was telling me. No book or course can explain what this intangible force is. You'll know it when you feel it.

Without a checklist, I relied on the intangible energy I felt throughout the journey. There was a certain emotion I felt when I was baking challah, dancing salsa, mentoring students, catering birthday parties with panini-pressed donuts, and even learning computer coding that inspired me to continue moving in that direction. After sharing these energies with those around me, I received it back in ways I didn't think possible, via introductions to mentors, projects, and new opportunities. These were the flowers in the fields—the experiences that led me to the next step.

Focus on the Present

As someone who has always thought about the next flower(s), I have realized that this not only takes away from the present moment but prevents me from understanding how to best navigate the problems and issues that arise day to day.

While working at B4, Dansk, and Revoire, I tried to work on ten different projects at a time and was burning myself out. Although my meditation and outside activities helped me get better about physically slowing down, my mind was always in fight or flight, stressing about work or thinking about what task I needed to complete to continue cross-pollinating. About two years ago, I met someone at the Indie Author Book

Conference who said something very profound regarding this tendency and how it could prevent me from ever finishing *NewBee* to begin with.

Since starting my book project, I have been following JP, an author coach who teaches authors about self-publishing and building their businesses. When I heard that she was going to be at the Indie Author Conference in Philadelphia, I knew that I needed to go, not only to learn more about the publishing process but for the chance to continue my public relations and meet her. The conference was filled with many great workshops that included traditional marketing, website building, printing, public speaking, and more. My busy-bee mind was fascinated and also overwhelmed by the many responsibilities required of authors. How did they concentrate on getting their books out there, knowing all the tasks they needed to juggle?

During a break, I spotted JP talking to a group of attendees in the corner of the lobby. I tiptoed my way over and waited until she was free. *What was I was going to say?*

"Thank you for being here. I've been reading your work for two years," I started, stalling until something hit me. Then, boom.

"All of the information in the conference is amazing and overwhelming at the same time. As an author, how do you balance marketing, creating the website, coordinating your speaking events, evaluating different options, and working on the actual book?"

"Where are you with the book?" she asked.

"I have the name, the website, the marketing materials, I've spoken to printers, designed the cover ..."

"What about the actual manuscript; is it done yet?"

"No, I'm still working on it," I told her.

"Okay, until you finish that manuscript, don't do anything else. Without that, you have no book, and there is nothing else to work on. Focus on the most important task in front of you," she said. It was a metaphor for an overarching lesson I needed to apply in my life.

While pollinating, it's easy to get swept up by the conferences, books, projects, and even work assignments that we feel the need to complete. I kept myself busy by checking these boxes, telling myself that completing these tasks would help me get closer to my goal. In reality, most of the activities I filled my life with were distractions from the task in front of me. Without a finished manuscript, there was no book I could get published. Without sufficient standardized test scores, students can't get into their dream college. Without passing the bar, lawyers can't practice law. You get the point.

Focus on the tasks that you must do *now*. The next steps will reveal themselves.

"When you are holding that finished manuscript in your hand, you will know exactly how to take the next steps," She told me.

Systems engineers call this concept the "critical path." In our world, critical-path activities advance processes from start to finish. Since we are able to clearly define the start and finish of repeatable processes, engineers look at the specific steps that lead to the next ones. Life doesn't work out in the same way. It's impossible for us to draw out the critical path of life, especially when we are constantly venturing into newfound territory way outside of our comfort zones. A concept akin to this is that of adjacent possibility.

Discovering All the Adjacent Possibilities

In *Where Good Ideas Come From*, Steven Johnson defines the adjacent possible as "a kind of shadow future, hovering on the edges of the present state of things, a map of all the ways in which the present can reinvent itself." Throughout my journey, I was consistently surprised by the shadow futures that existed at the edges of the different experiences I pursued. After falling in love with restaurants and receiving advice about pursuing an engineering degree, I started thinking about which degree would support combining the two fields. Systems engineering seemed like a logical choice, which then required me to ask how it could be applied in the real world, which led to using what I learned in the programming class for the nightclub. Each present moment pivoted into the next adjacent possibility without me being conscious of its existence.

Creating guest-tracking technology for the hospitality industry was a future I didn't realize existed. Pursuing that avenue led to being inspired to use automated systems to manage my bakery business, discovering tech consulting, and ultimately, creating roles within the restaurant world that enabled me to combine my skills to create multiple dream jobs. Even if these roles led to extremely dark moments in my life, I still had the chance to live through those feelings and recognize critical lessons for my own development.

The adjacent possibilities are never apparent. They are shadow futures that are only discovered when we put ourselves out there, having faith that the next steps in our lives exist.

Honey Is the Unique Mosaic of our Life

As NewBees, each of our sets of hopes, dreams, passions, skills, and interests is unique. There is no standard path that any of us should be taking. No one person, book, job, or experience will have the answers for you. Without an instruction manual or playbook, we must navigate the fields of life, extract pollen from every moment we live through, and create our own path. We can use the concept of vision boards to filter what interests us and direct ourselves on our journey.

One of the first ideas described in *NewBee* was the concept of how vision boards can be used to manifest our deepest wishes. The idea is that everything on our vision board one day becomes a component of our lives. As we go through the different experiences of our lives, we extract nectar—learn lessons—that become our honey.

The hexagon is the shape chosen to symbolize the honeycomb. The pattern on the front of the book and of each chapter is made up of several overlapping hexagons representing honey. Each comb is split into multiple components, making up the plethora of lessons that can be combined with the takeaways from other experiences. The sum of our learnings across all the hexes create highly valuable insights and skill sets, specific to each one of us. Our vision boards manifest into the mosaic of our lives, with numerous lessons learned as we connect the dots. The design captures the essence of how we develop a unique point of view.

As JP predicted, I now know exactly what I need to do now that I have finished my manuscript. Looking over my own mosaic, I am able to visualize the next steps-the adjacent possibility-that I will manifest in my life.

Creating My Category

Before I started working at Revoire, the restaurant technology startup, I was given another book to read that was about category design, the discipline of creating new products and services, titling them with a unique name, and teaching people a new way of solving problems. The book was meant to serve as an introduction to the category that Revoire was trying to create—connected restaurant technology. We eventually hired the team that wrote the book to come and teach us about creating narratives around our products and services, to educate the restaurant world about the benefits of this new way of operating.

The team started their workshops around the time I returned from the trip to the Poconos, where I discovered the message that I wanted *NewBee* to represent. On the second day of our workshops, the team announced the name for the category we were creating—Restaurant OS. While we were discussing how our technology was going to change the game, I couldn't stop thinking about how the idea of curating the experience of our lives using Cross-Pollination Design could help people answer the question of how to expand the search for fulfillment beyond their careers, into the holistic experience of life. That day, I invented the name of the category I was going to create.

Now that I've finished synthesizing my journey, it's time to figure out how I am going to introduce the world to Cross-Pollination Design.

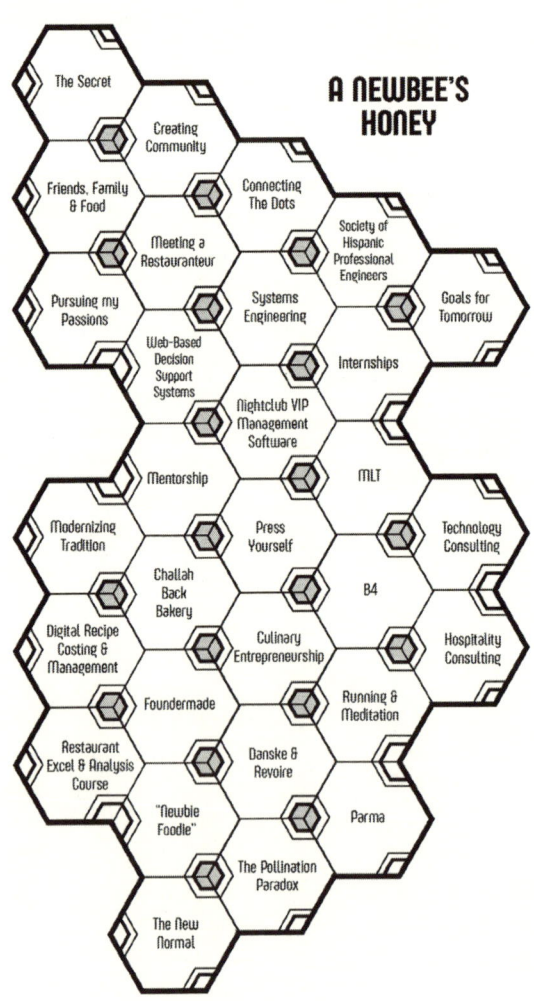

A NEWBEE'S HONEY

The Secret
Creating Community
Friends, Family & Food
Connecting The Dots
Meeting a Restauranteur
Society of Hispanic Professional Engineers
Pursuing my Passions
Systems Engineering
Goals for Tomorrow
Web-Based Decision Support Systems
Internships
Nightclub VIP Management Software
Mentorship
MLT
Modernizing Tradition
Press Yourself
Technology Consulting
Challah Back Bakery
B4
Digital Recipe Costing & Management
Culinary Entrepreneurship
Hospitality Consulting
Foundermade
Running & Meditation
Restaurant Excel & Analysis Course
Danske & Revoire
"Newbie Foodie"
Parma
The Pollination Paradox
The New Normal

SO, WHAT'S NEXT?

Thank you for coming on this journey with me.

As mentioned in the conclusion of my book, I have decided to face all fears and leap into entrepreneurship. There are two big projects on the table. The first will involve the exploration of how cross-pollination principles can be applied to help create change in our lives. I am fascinated by the idea of how people have cross-pollinated in a world that has been shut down—how people have completely reinvented their lives to accommodate the great changes that have manifested. I hope to share these lessons through a podcast, blog, or perhaps another book.

The second project is an introductory course on restaurant analytics and technology, meant to educate restaurant professionals who wish to learn about how technology is used to analyze the performance of their business. No matter how drastically a global pandemic will enforce change upon our society, professionals who improve their technology literacy will be able to understand how tools can be used to serve our guests in a safe environment, while monitoring their business. While the hospitality industry has forever changed, it isn't going away any time soon.

More info on both projects can be found on my website, www.ernestomandowsky.com.

I'd love to hear any thoughts and comments you might have! Please send me a note at book@crosspollinationdesign.com.

Thank you,
Ernesto Mandowsky

ACKNOWLEDGEMENTS

The list of people I must thank for being a positive force in my life is long, however these are a few that I would like to highlight with a special shoutout.

Ma-Thank you for inspiring me to keep doing my public relations!

Papi-Thank you for teaching me to be patient and to use The Secret to manifest my desires.

Thank you to the rest of my family who have shared their love with me throughout the journey.

Gracias Yrenea por todo lo que me enseñastes de como amar mi familia y mis amigos

Lexx-Thank you for putting up with my frying garlic and onions everyday at 7 AM for 3 years of our lives. And, for letting me turn our apartment into a ratchet bakery.

Kevin-Thanks for sparking the Fuego in me to dance, to make moves and to hustle.

Mitch, Brian and the Shonz-Thank you for volunteering yourselves to share in random facetime rants on the latest crazy idea I've had.

Schwazz-Thanks for putting up with me as a roommate for 5 years, listening to my violin concertos, smelling the burnt ovens, and offering your sensei wisdom.

Michael D, Matt B, Steph D, Wally G, Doug S, and LP-thank you for being my tight knit support group while at B4 and beyond.

Lauren & the Denowitz Fam -Thank you for welcoming me with open arms during the most chaotic year of my life. Your support was immensely appreciated.

Patrick-the OG "Newbie Foodie"-Thank you for teaching me how to improve my storytelling.

Cheryl-Thank you for opening up my mind to different perspectives.

Hannah and Maialen-Thank you for believing in me over the years, and for your friendship.

Whit-Thank you for being a friend and mentor. Your seat will always be waiting for you at the table with a freshly-baked pan de bono waiting.

Jens and Shu-Thank you for giving me the opportunity to dive into the food & beverage industry and learn how the role of technology systems and analysis come together to help restaurants succeed.

Jennie-Thank you for helping me create such a beautiful design that captures the essence of what it means to create your honey through cross-pollination

Thank you, Headspace, Calm, and every other meditation platform that is out there making life, less stressful.

Thank you, King Arthur Bakery, for creating ingredients that empowers everyone in America to create delicious baked goods.

Thank you Team BookBaby for helping me organize myself during this publication process.

Thank you to all my Challah Backers who have supported my carb-loaded baking education.

Thank you to all the people that I have met throughout the years, cross-pollinating throughout my jobs, courses, and conferences, that have given me the confidence to continue creating my honey